Chic Friendship: Adult Creations with Hemp, Thread, and Other Materials

Discover Elegant Styles for Friendship Bracelets with Natural and Boho Chic Materials

COPY PERMISSION: The written instructions, photographs, designs, patterns, and projects in this publication are intended for the personal use of the reader and may be reproduced for that purpose only. Any other use, especially commercial use, is forbidden under law without the written permission of the copyright holder. Every effort has been made to ensure that all information in this book is accurate. However, due to differing conditions, tools, and individual skills, neither the author nor publisher can be responsible for any injuries, losses, or other damages which may result from the use of the information in this book.

INFORMATION: All rights reserved. All images in this book have been reproduced with the knowledge and prior consent of the artists concerned and no responsibility is accepted by producer, publisher, or printer for any infringement of copyright or otherwise, arising from the contents of this publication. Every effort has been made to ensure that credits accurately comply with information supplied.

WARNING: Due to the components used in this craft, children under 8 years of age should not have access to materials or supplies. Under rare circumstances components of products could cause serious or fatal injury. Neither New Design Originals, Suzanne McNeill, the product manufacturer, or the supplier is responsible.

NOTE: The use of products and trademark names is for informational purposes only, with no intention of infringement upon those trademarks.

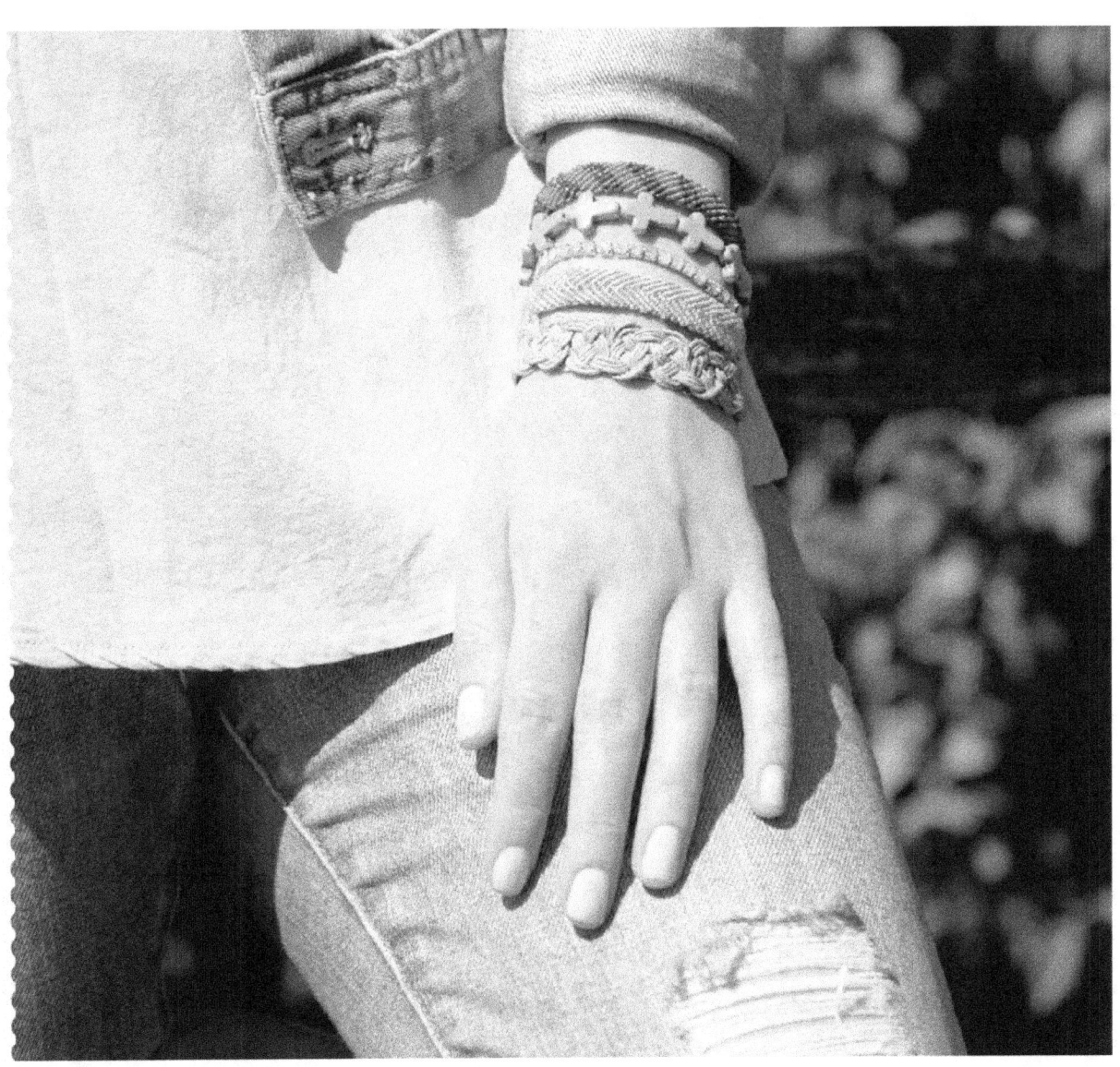

COMBINE A RELAXED HIPPIE VIBE WITH YOUR OWN SENSE OF STYLE.

CELEBRATE THE THINGS YOU LOVE BY MAKING YOUR BRACELET DESIGNS A REFLECTION OF THEM—WHETHER IT'S MUSIC AND ART, SAND AND SURF, FRIENDS AND FAMILY, OR A LITTLE BIT OF EVERYTHING!

BRING WHAT YOU LOVE INTO THESE DESIGNS, WHETHER IT'S VIBRANT COLORS OR SOPHISTICATED FLAIR, AND YOU'LL LOVE TO WEAR THEM THAT MUCH MORE.

TABLE OF CONTENTS

FRIENDSHIP DESIGNS

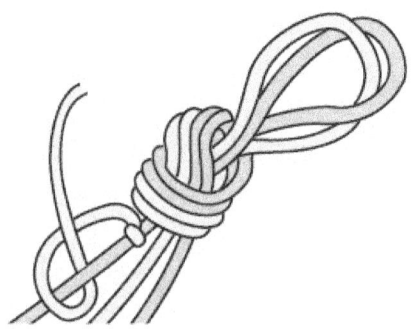

The Basics

French Twist or Chinese Staircase

Three-Strand Braid

Four-Strand Flat Braid

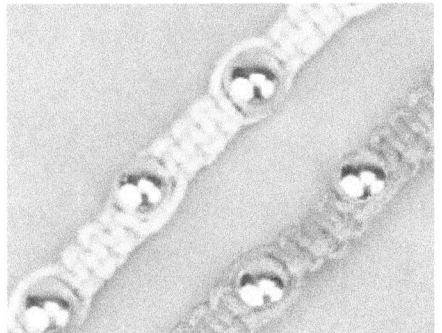

Square Knot

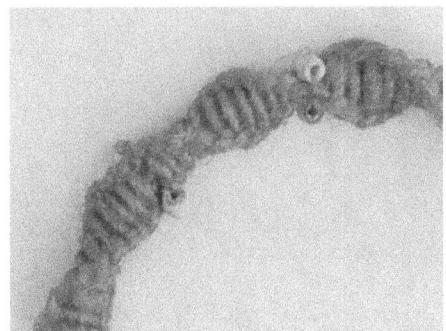

Half Knot Twist

Stripes

Crisscross Stripes

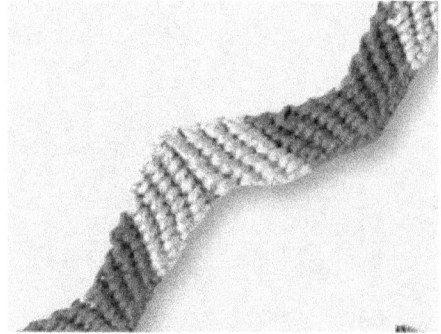

Zigzag Stripes

Symmetrical Chevrons

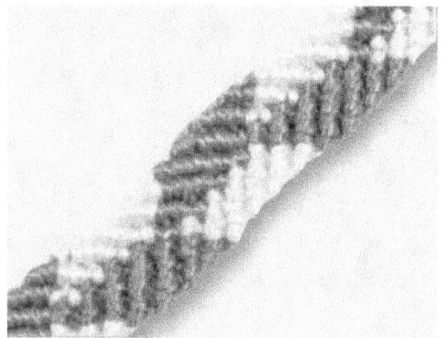

Asymmetrical Chevrons

Single Waves

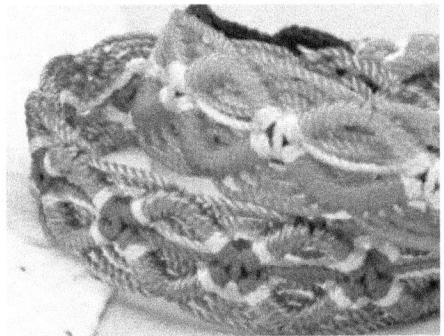

Double Waves

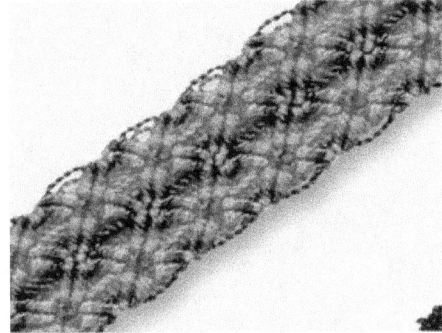

Dual Double Waves

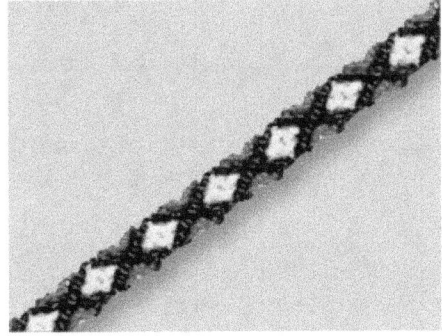

Small Diamonds

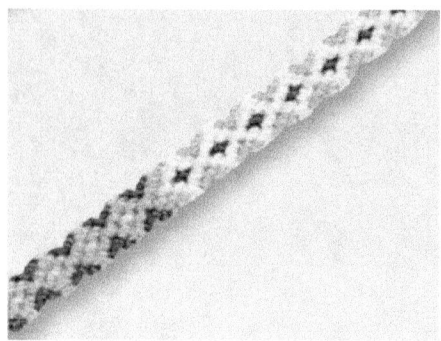

Alternating Color Diamonds

Wide Alternating Color Diamonds

Diamonds in Diamonds

HEMP DESIGNS

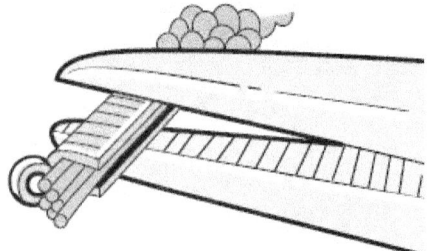

The Basics

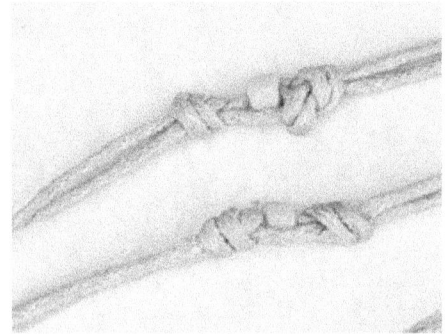

Overhand Knot

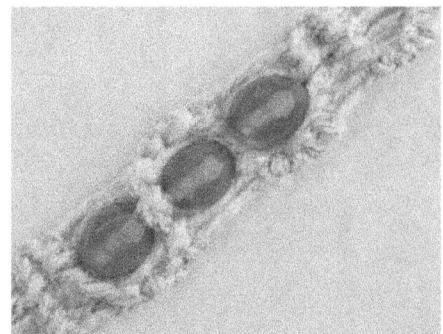

Half Hitch Knot

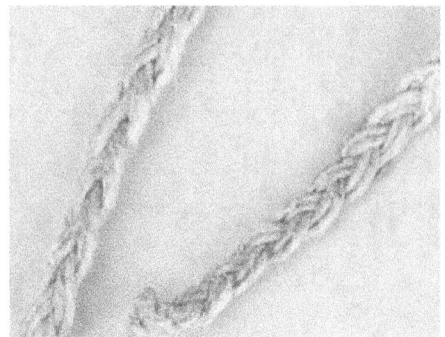

Three-Strand Braid

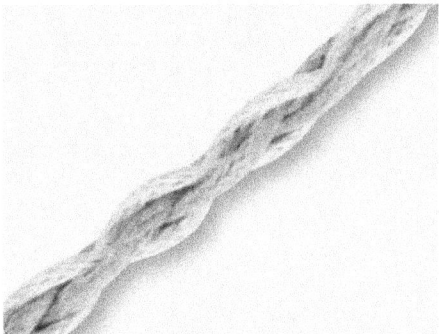

Four-Strand Round Braid

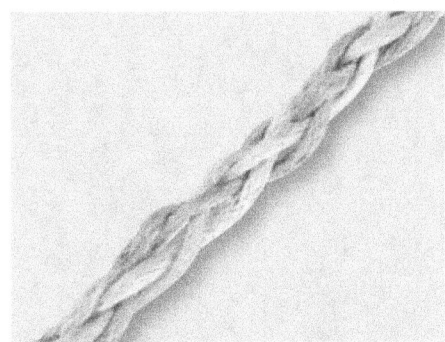

Five-Strand Braid

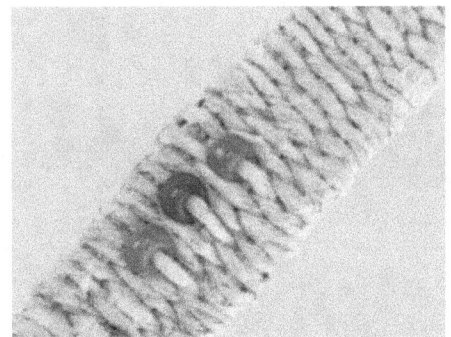

Woven Bands

Josephine Knot

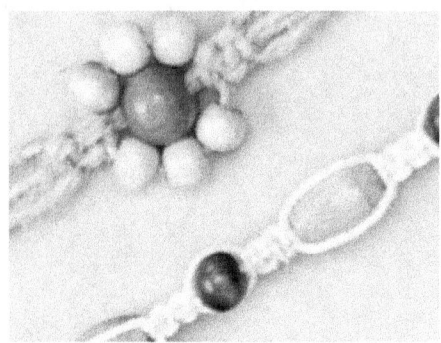

Square Knot

Half Knot Twist

MORE STYLISH DESIGNS

Bungee Cord

Plastic Lace

Lightweight Paracord

More Great Ideas

FRIENDSHIP DESIGNS

Bracelets knotted from embroidery floss likely bring to mind childhood memories of school and recess. By incorporating updated colors and creative modifications to match your taste, however, you can transform these designs from middle-school memories to current pieces you are proud to display. Whether you're going for a boho chic, mod, or all-out fashionista look, these designs will allow you to create exactly what you want. To get the hang of things, start with the basic instructions for each pattern to learn how to organize your strands and the order in which to knot them to create your design. Then, get inspired by the hundreds of ways in which you can customize your projects to make them your very own. From color to closures to beads, there are endless ways to make these bracelets as unique as you!

THE BASICS

Unless otherwise stated, use 36" (91.5cm) strands of embroidery floss or No. 3 or No. 5 pearl cotton thread for each color in a design. For designs with two strands of the same color, use 72" (183cm) strands doubled over unless otherwise stated.

To begin

Tie the strands for your bracelet together using an overhand knot with a ½" (1.5cm) loop at the top. For bracelets using 36" (91.5cm) strands, double over the first few inches to form the loop. For bracelets using 72" (183cm) strands, fold the strands in half to form the loop. Secure the knotted end of your bracelet to your workspace with tape.

KEEPING YOUR KNOTS STRAIGHT

Remember, the terms "forward" and "backward" refer to the directions in which your strands move. Forward knots move from left to right, like when you read. Backward knots move from right to left. Terms like "forward-backward" and "backward-forward" might seem confusing at first; just do exactly what the name says and you'll be fine! For forward-backward knots, tie a forward knot, and then a backward one with the same strand. For backward-forward knots, tie a backward knot, and then a forward knot.

Basic forward knot

Bring the leftmost strand over and then under the strand immediately to the right of it. Pull the end of the working strand through the loop that has formed. Pull the knot up firmly against the overhand knot at the end of the bracelet. This is called a half hitch knot.

Repeat, tying a second half hitch knot using the same strand. Pull the second knot up firmly against the first. You will see that the strands switch places. Always tie two half hitches for each knot before moving on to the next strand.

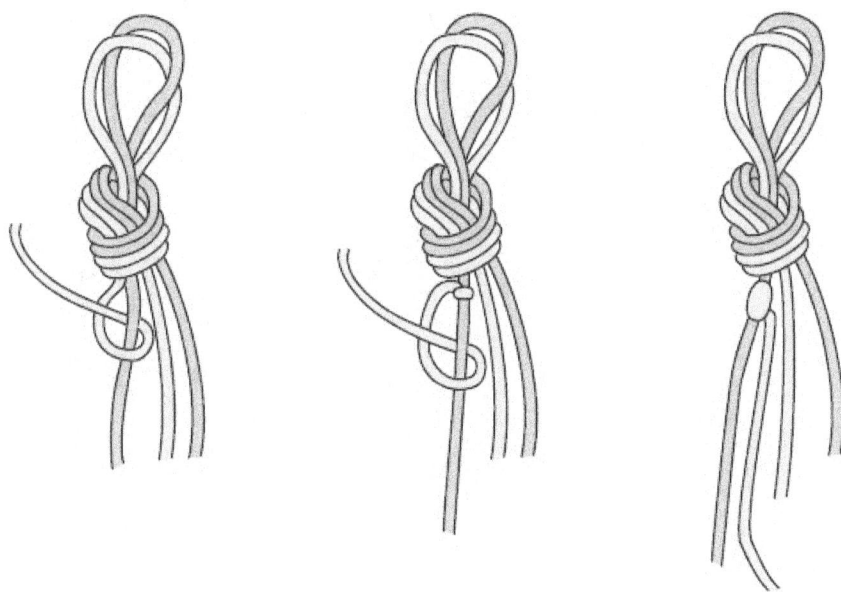

Basic backward knot

A backward knot is the reverse of a forward knot and is tied onto the strand to the left to move the knot backward. Follow the illustrations to tie a backward knot. Remember, always tie two half hitches for each knot before moving on to the next strand.

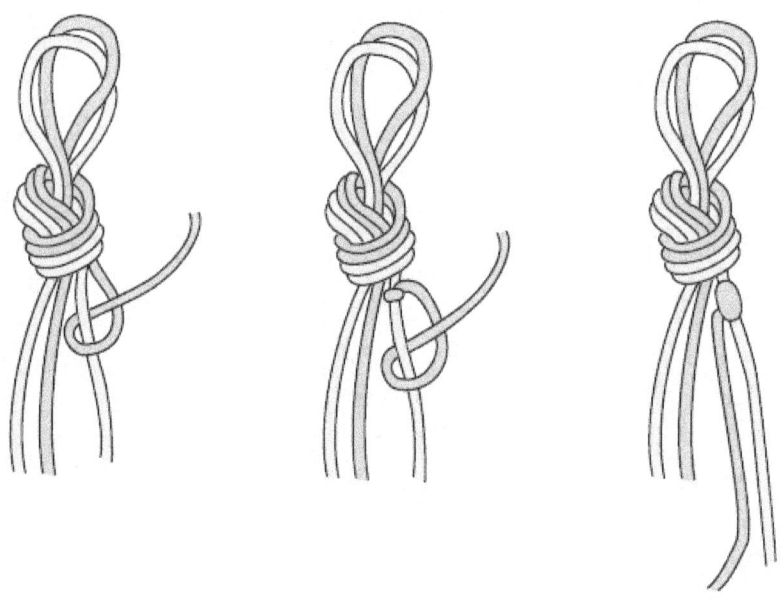

Forward-backward knot

Tie a forward knot with the leftmost strand. This moves the strand to the right. Then, using the same strand, tie a backward knot. This moves the strand back where it started.

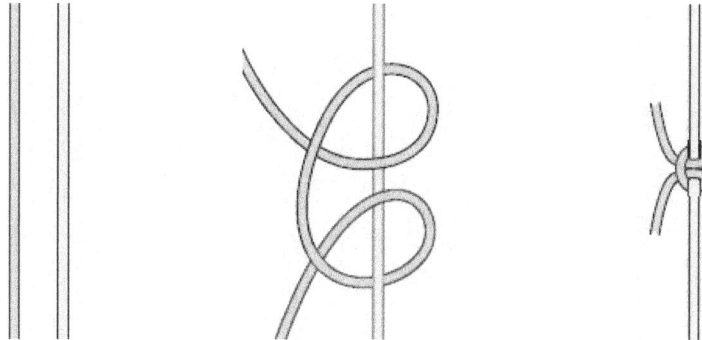

Backward-forward knot

Tie a backward knot with the rightmost strand. This moves the strand to the left. Then, using the same strand, tie a forward knot. This moves the strand back where it started.

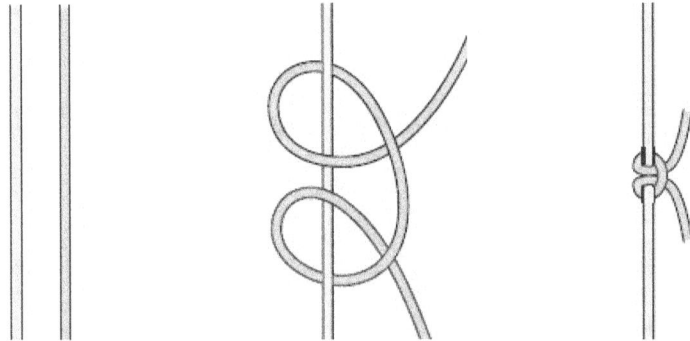

To end

Depending on the number of threads your bracelet uses and your desired look, there are several ways you can finish your bracelet.

Option 1: Divide the strands at the end of the bracelet into three groups and braid them together. Secure with an overhand knot and trim.

Option 2: Divide the strands at the end of the bracelet into six groups. Braid the three left groups together and the three right groups together. Secure with overhand knots and trim.

Option 3: Tie all the strands at the end of the bracelet together in an overhand knot. Use the loose ends to tie the bracelet onto your wrist.

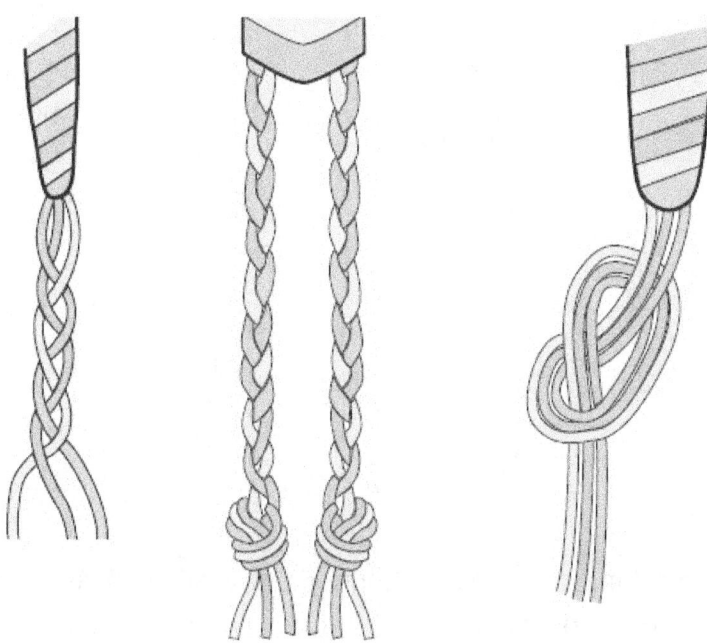

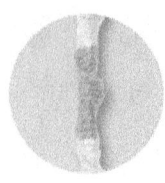 # FRENCH TWIST or CHINESE STAIRCASE

By using a repeating half hitch knot, you can create an overall design known as a French Twist or Chinese Staircase. Start with seven 72" (183cm) strands doubled over for fourteen strands total. Tie the strands together using an overhand knot with a ½" (1.5cm) loop at the top. Secure the knotted end of the bracelet to your work surface.

1 Beginning with the color strand of your choice, tie ten half hitch knots around the other strands. You can use either a forward knot or a backward knot (see this page), whichever is easier for you to make.

2 After you've completed the first ten knots, select a different color strand and use it to tie ten half hitch knots around the other strands. Continue until you reach the desired length, alternating colors as you wish.

THREE-STRAND BRAID

Start with three groups of strands. You can use anything from three 36" (91.5cm) single strands for a thin braid to six 72" (183cm) strands doubled over to form a thicker braid with three groups of four strands.

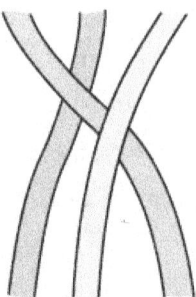

1 Tie the ends of the strands together using an overhand knot with a ½" (1.5cm) loop at the top. Bring the left group of strands over the center strands so the left group is now in the center. Then, bring the right group of strands over the center strands so the right group is now in the center.

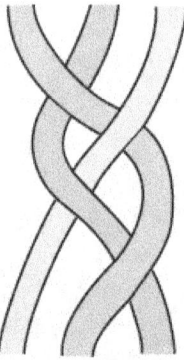

2 Continue until you reach the desired length.

Give this classic design a simple twist by changing the number of strands you use and selecting coordinating colors. The top bracelet uses nine strands, the next two use six strands, and the bottom bracelet uses four strands.

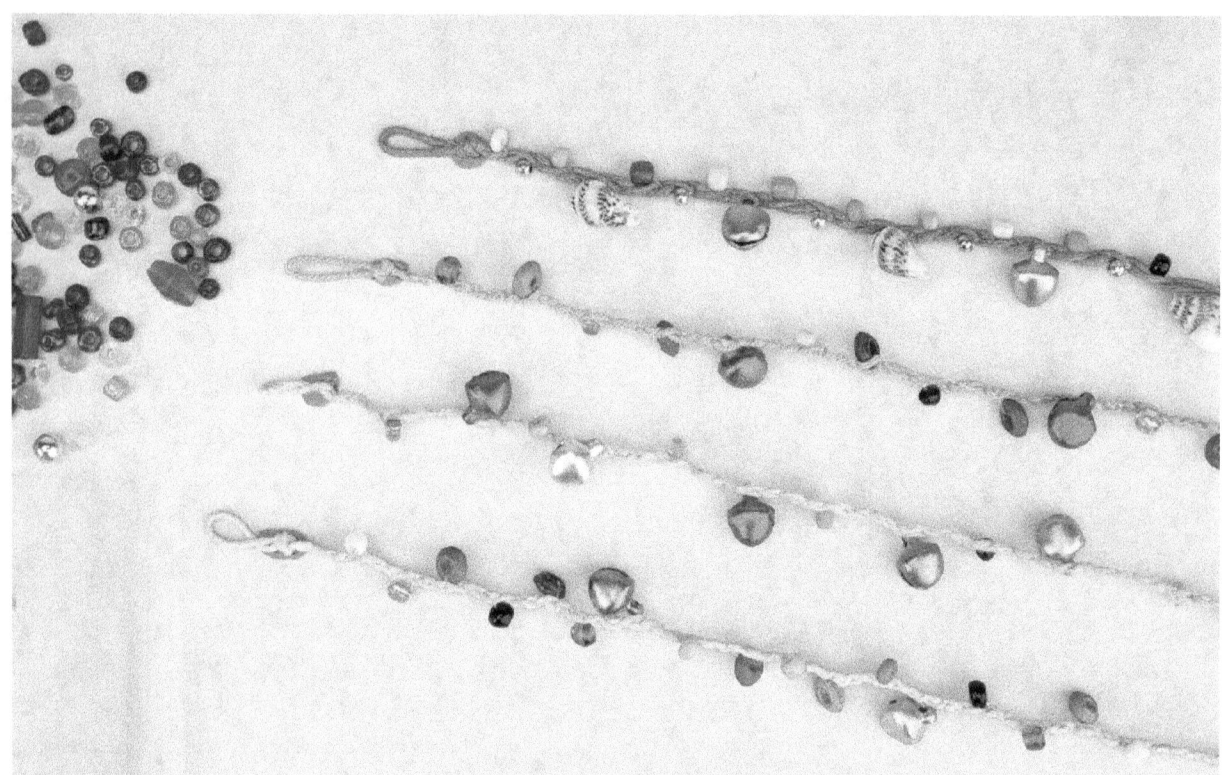

Small seed beads, shells, and bells make perfect embellishments for tiny braids. Make a full set in tons of colors that you can stack high on your wrist.

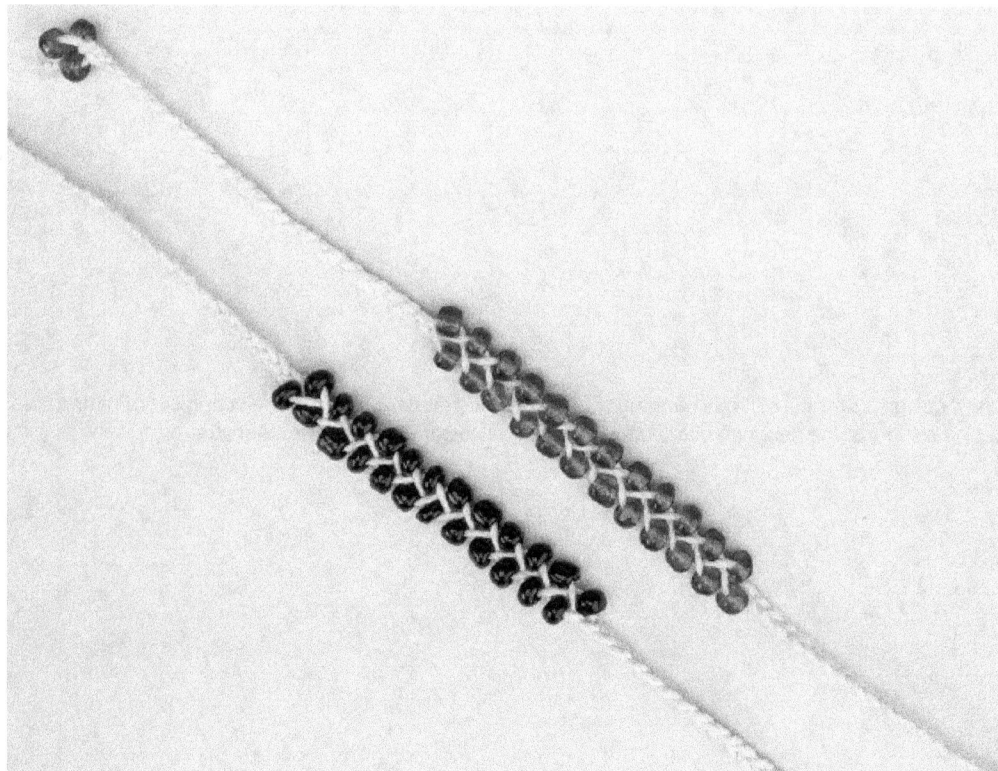

Enhance a simple braid by making a beaded focal section. Add beads to the outer strands as you braid them until the focal section reaches the length you desire.

FOUR-STRAND FLAT BRAID

Start with two groups of 36" (91.5cm) strands. The design shown uses two groups with three strands each, but you can use more or less strands in each group as you desire.

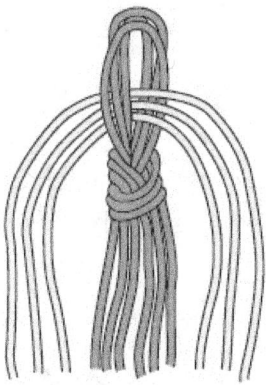

1 Fold one group of strands in half and tie an overhand knot with a ½" (1.5cm) loop at the top. Thread the other group of strands through the loop and center them over the overhand knot.

2 Bring the outer right group of strands over the group immediately to the left. Repeat with the outer left group of strands, bringing it over the group immediately to the right. Bring the center left group over the center right group. Keep the strands in each group side by side as you work the braid.

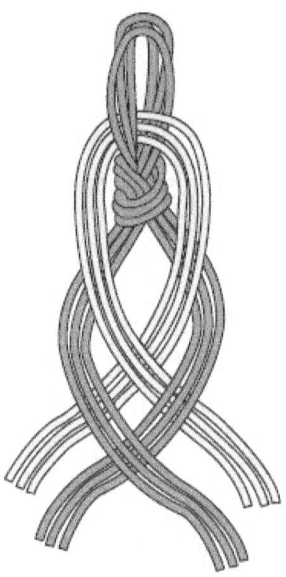

3 Repeat with the new outer strands, crossing the left group over the right group at the center of the bracelet. Continue until you reach the desired length.

SQUARE KNOT

Start with two 72" (183cm) strands doubled over for four strands total.

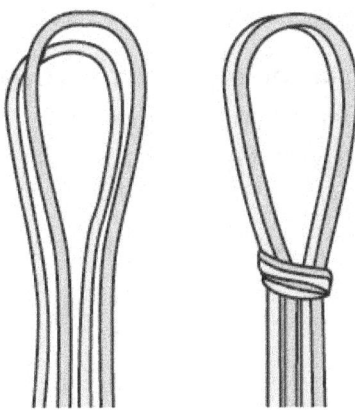

1 Arrange the strands to create the pattern you desire. To create a dual-color bracelet, make sure the outermost strands are two different colors. Tie the strands together using an overhand knot with a ½" (1.5cm) loop at the top.

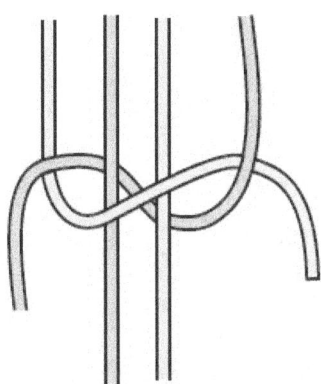

2 Bring the outer right strand under the center strands and over the outer left strand. Bring the outer left strand over the center strands and under the outer right strand.

3 To finish the square knot, bring the outer right strand over the center strands and under the outer left strand. Bring the outer left strand under the center strands and over the outer right strand. Repeat Steps 2–3 until you reach the desired length.

ALTERNATING COLORS

To alternate colors, use two strands of the same color for the outer strands and two strands of the same color for the inner strands. Work several square knots with the outer strands. To switch colors, bring the inner strands to the outside and work several square knots with them.

To create a dual-color alternating bracelet, arrange the strands so the colors alternate. Tie several square knots with the outer strands. To switch colors, bring two strands of the same color to the outside and work several square knots with them.

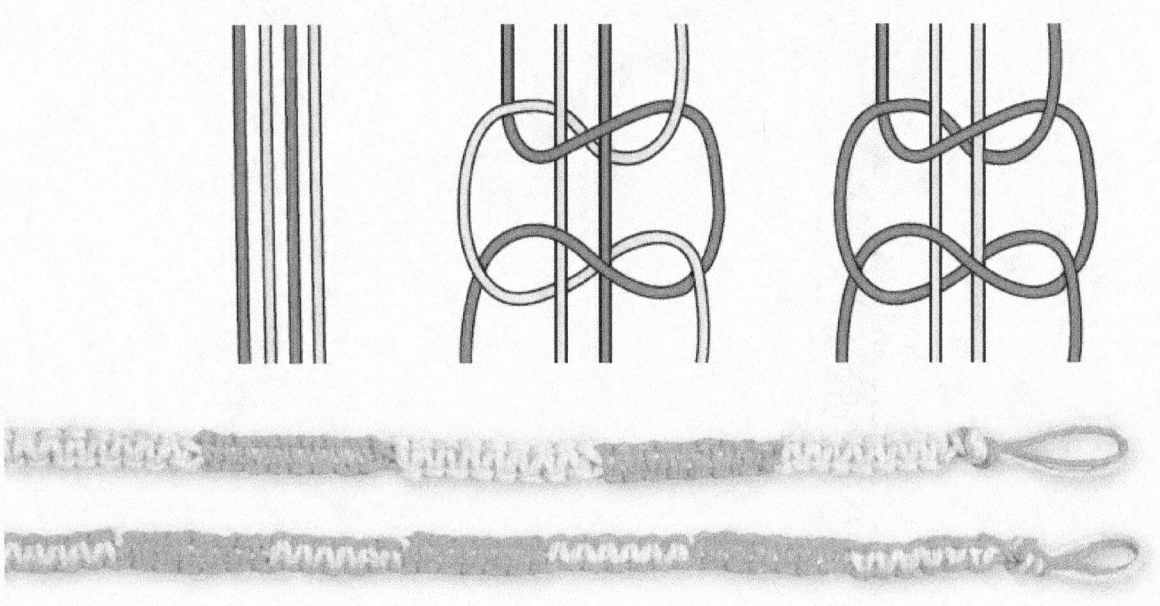

ADDING BEADS

Add small beads (like seed beads or 2mm round beads) to the outer working strands as you tie your square knots. You can also add beads to one or both of the center strands as you work.

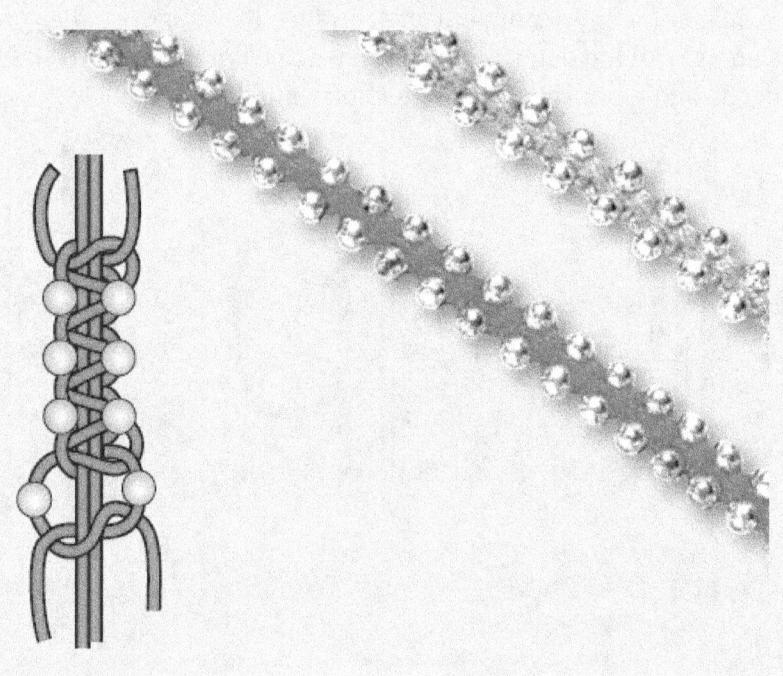

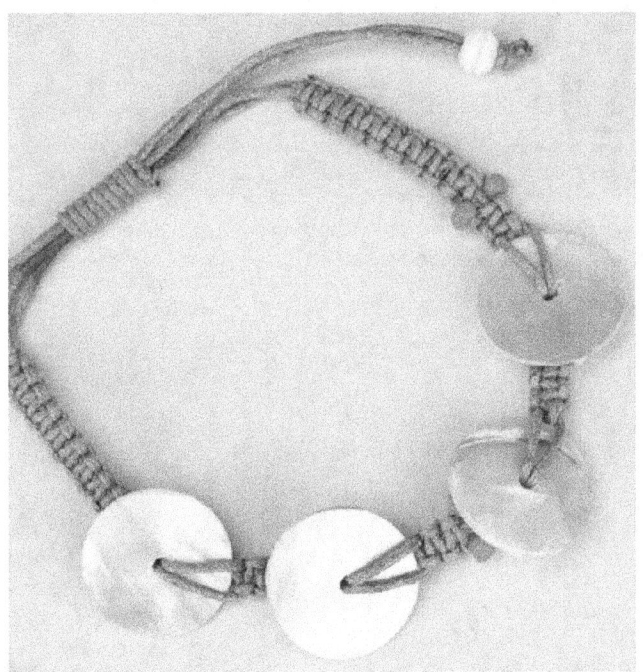

Get creative with beads! Add small beads to each working strand, or thread both working strands through large beads, like the disk beads here.

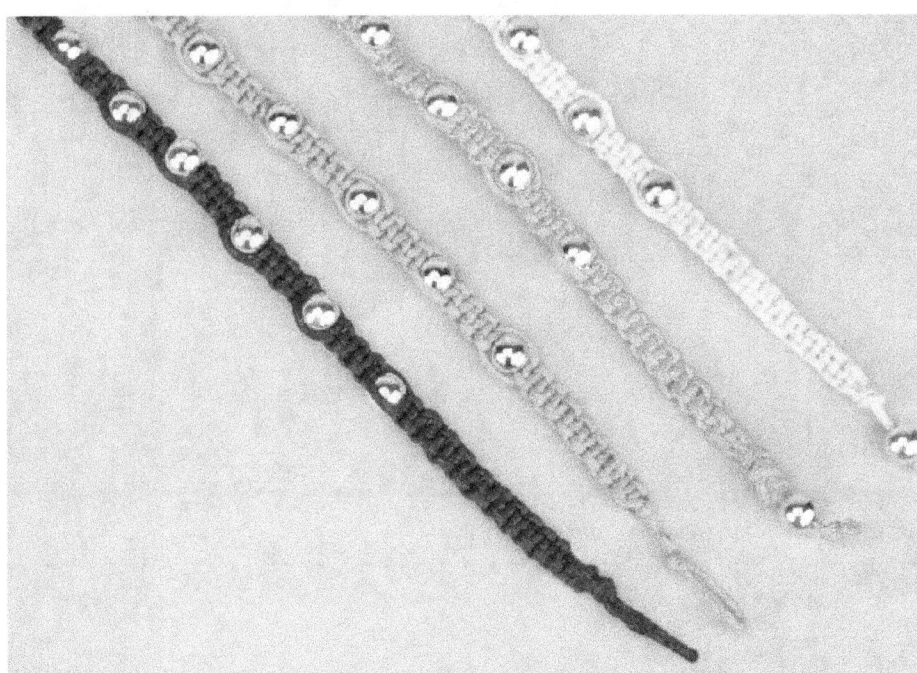

Add some bling with bright silver beads. Thread them onto the two center strands. Use bright, modern colors to make the silver pop.

To make this design, double over a base strand. Tie on two knotting strands in different colors. Tie knots around the base strand only with one color. Then, switch to the second color.

Use the full colors of the rainbow to create fun, bright designs!

Make cute flower designs by threading a center bead onto the two center strands and three petal beads onto each outer strand. This makes a perfect casual summer design.

HALF KNOT TWIST

This knot is called a half knot because it is the first half of a square knot. Start with two 72" (183cm) strands doubled over for four strands total.

1 Tie the strands together using an overhand knot with a ½" (1.5cm) loop at the top.

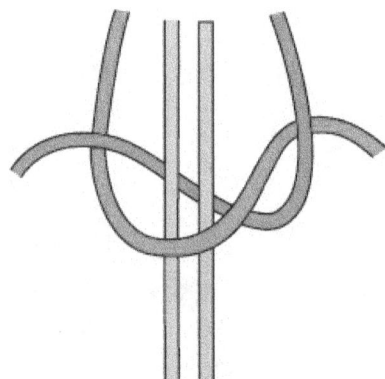

2 Bring the outer right strand under the center strands and over the outer left strand. Bring the outer left strand over the center strands and under the outer right strand.

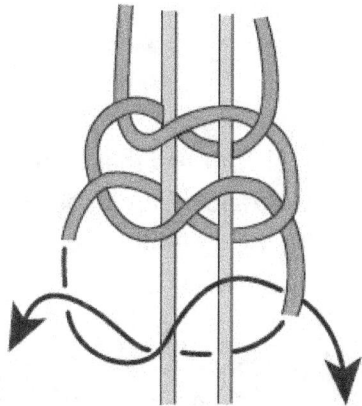

3 Repeat Step 2 until you reach the desired length. The outer right strand will always go under the center strands and over the outer left strand. The outer left strand will always go over the center strands and under the outer right strand.

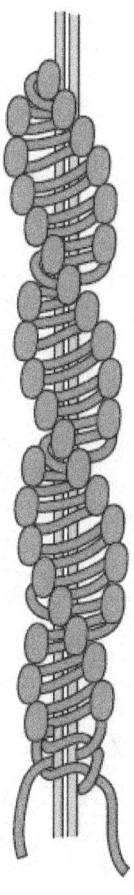

4 Tying a half knot will naturally cause the outer strands to twist around the center strands as you work, forming a spiral shape. Note that if you use two different colors for the outer strands, the colors at the center and the outside edges of the bracelet will alternate with every knot.

ADDING BEADS

To add beads to the center of the bracelet, thread them onto one or both center strands and tie half knots around them with the outer strands. To add beads to the outside edges of the bracelet, thread them onto one or both outer strands.

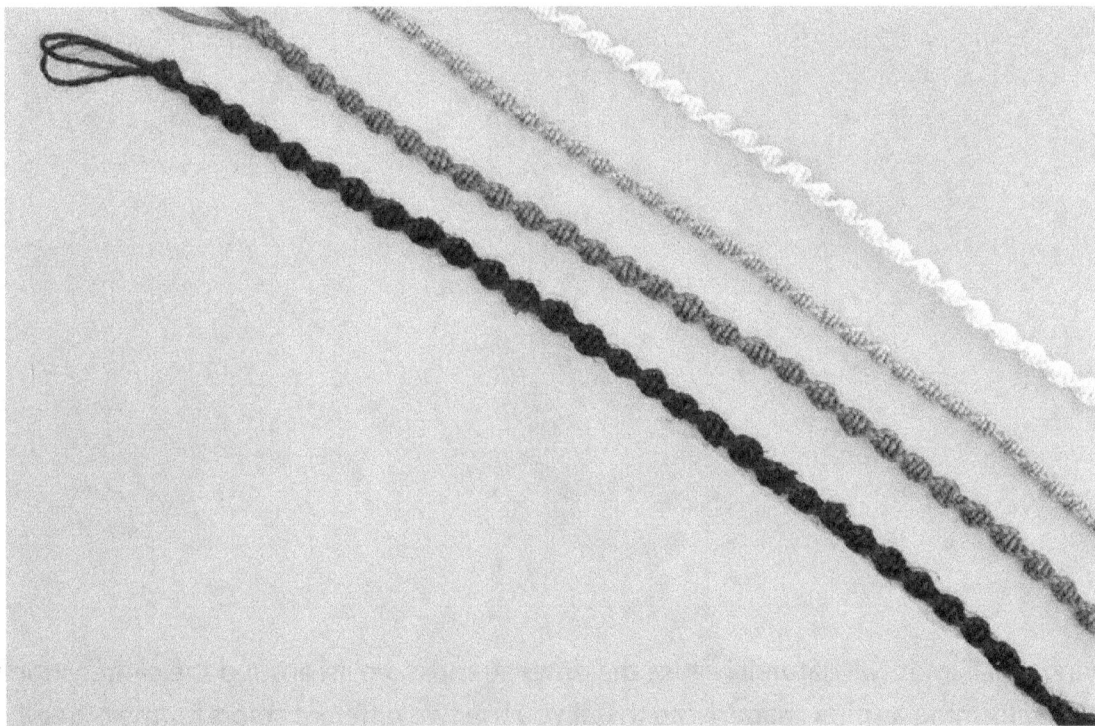

A set of bracelets in neutral colors will give any outfit a classic, upscale look. This set could easily dress up a T-shirt and jeans outfit.

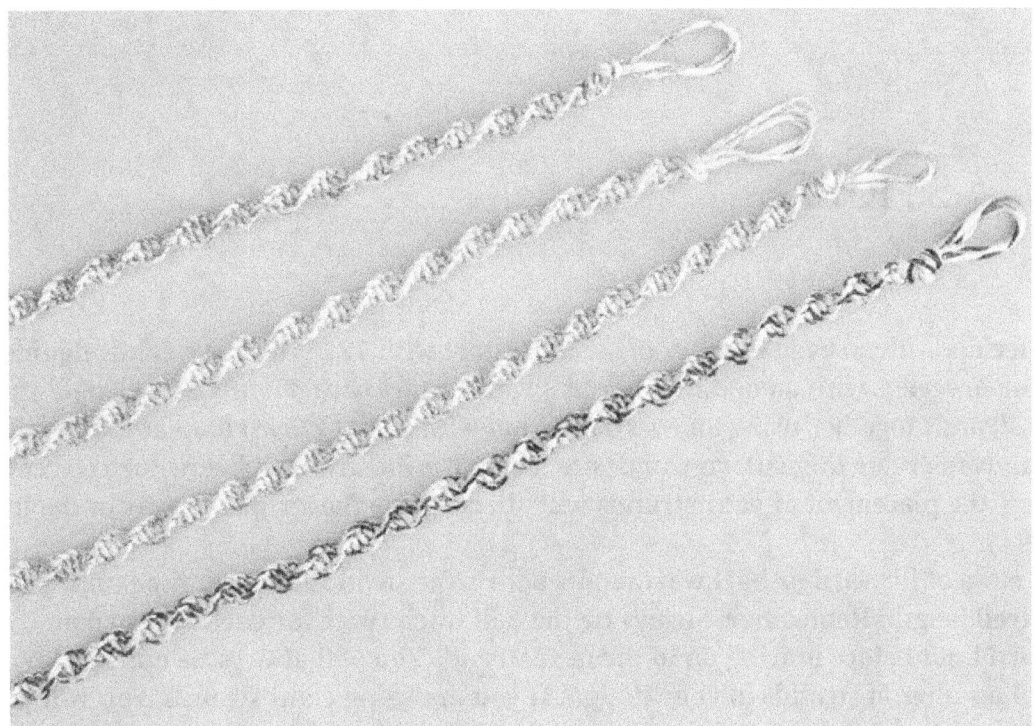

Try this knot with variegated or metallic floss. You'll love the results!

Beads always make a great addition to knotted jewelry designs. Add small beads to the outer working strands, or use large beads for a closure.

 # STRIPES

For bracelets with an even number of strands, start with 72" (183cm) strands doubled over. For bracelets with an odd number of strands, start with 36" (91.5cm) single strands. Tie the strands together using an overhand knot with a ½" (1.5cm) loop at the top. Arrange the strands to create the pattern you desire, using the illustrations below for reference. Note how the placement of your strands will affect where the stripes appear in the finished bracelet.

   Tie rows of forward or backward knots across the strands one at a time until you reach the desired length. Remember, always tie the half hitch twice for each forward or backward knot before moving on to the next strand. You will always tie one less knot than the total number of strands in your design. If you are using eight strands, you will tie seven knots across the bracelet. For four strands, you will tie three knots.

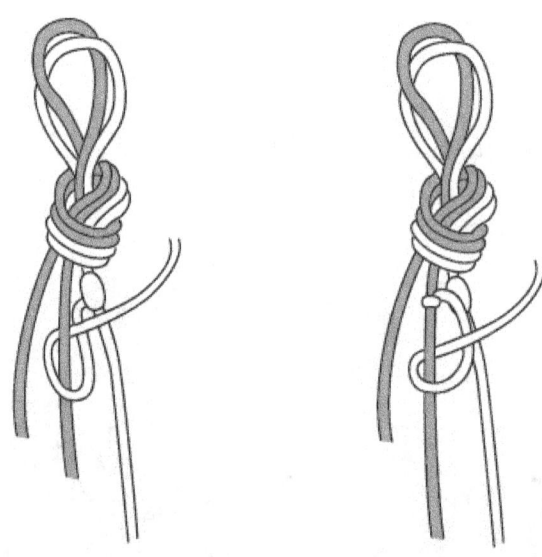

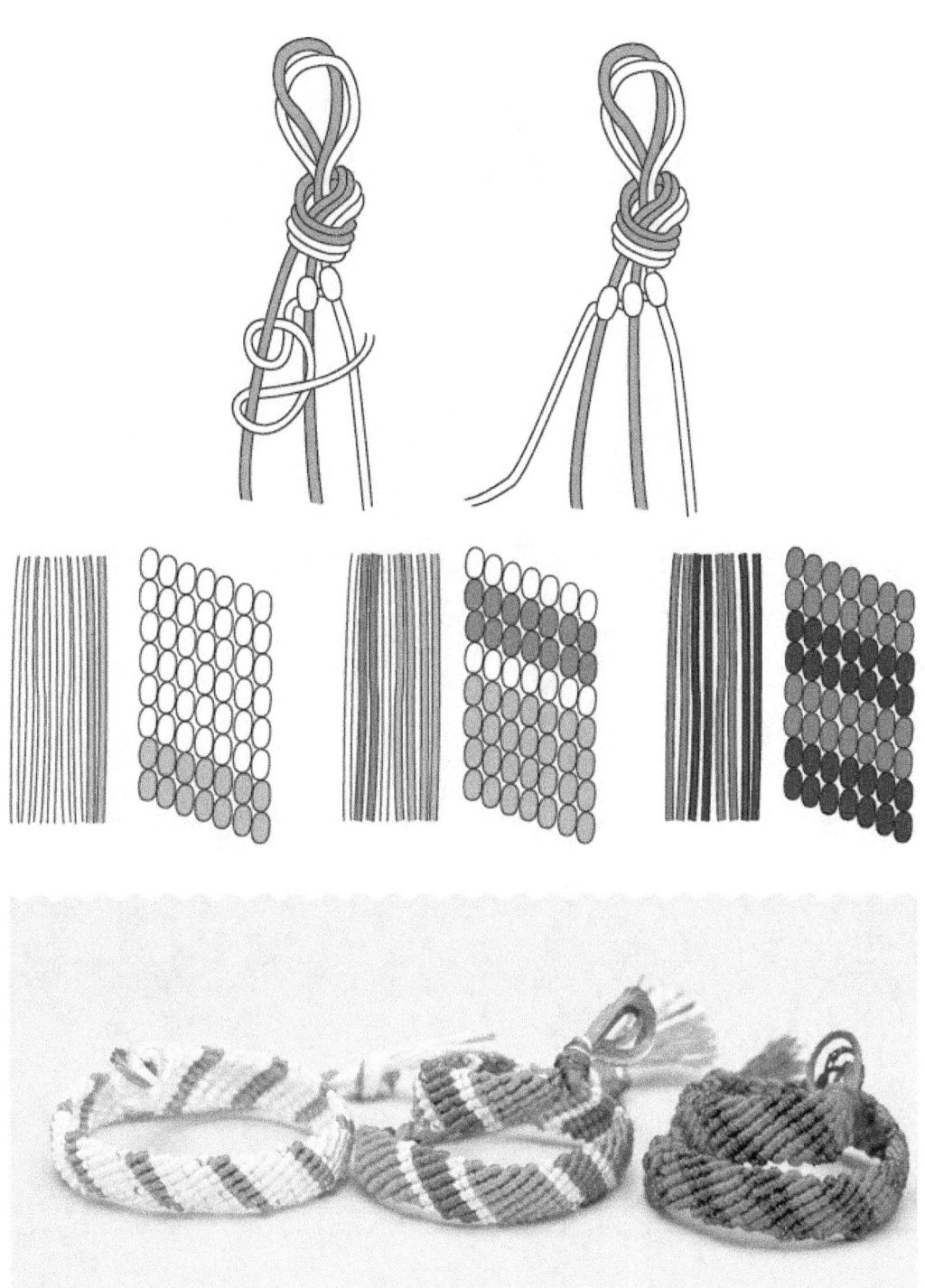

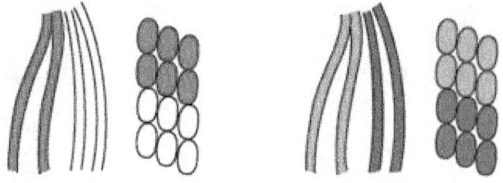

CRISSCROSS STRIPES

Start with four 72" (183cm) strands doubled over for eight strands total. Tie the strands together using an overhand knot with a ½" (1.5cm) loop at the top. Arrange the strands so the colors form a symmetrical pattern, using the illustration at the right for reference.

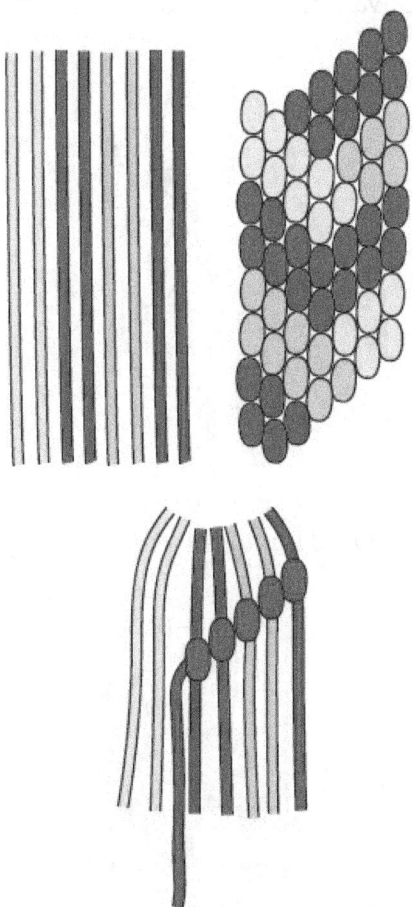

1 To begin, use the outer right strand to tie a row of five backward knots, working toward the center of the bracelet.

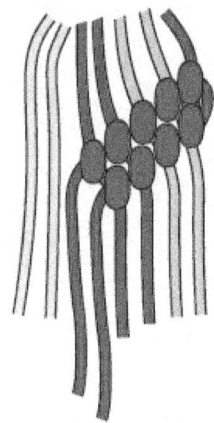

2 On the next row, tie four backward knots with the outer right strand.

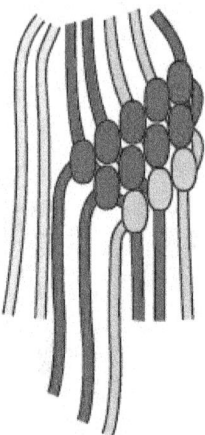

3 On the next row, tie three backward knots with the outer right strand.

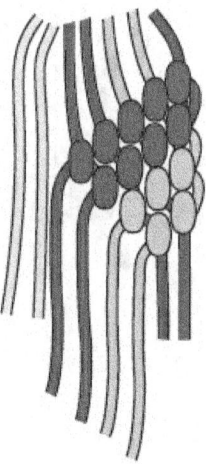

4 On the next row, tie two backward knots with the outer right strand.

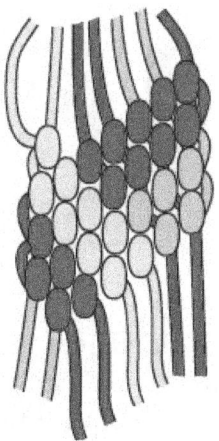

5 Repeat Steps 1–4 using forward knots to work from the left side of the bracelet toward the center. Start by tying five forward knots for the first row, four knots on the second row, three knots on the third row, and finally two knots on the fourth row.

6 Repeat Steps 1–5 until you reach the desired length.

ZIGZAG STRIPES

Start with four 72" (183cm) strands doubled over for eight strands total. Tie the strands together using an overhand knot with a ½" (1.5cm) loop at the top. Arrange the strands so the colors form a symmetrical pattern. To create a two-tone bracelet, place four strands of one color on the left side, and four strands of another color on the right side, as shown in the illustration at the right.

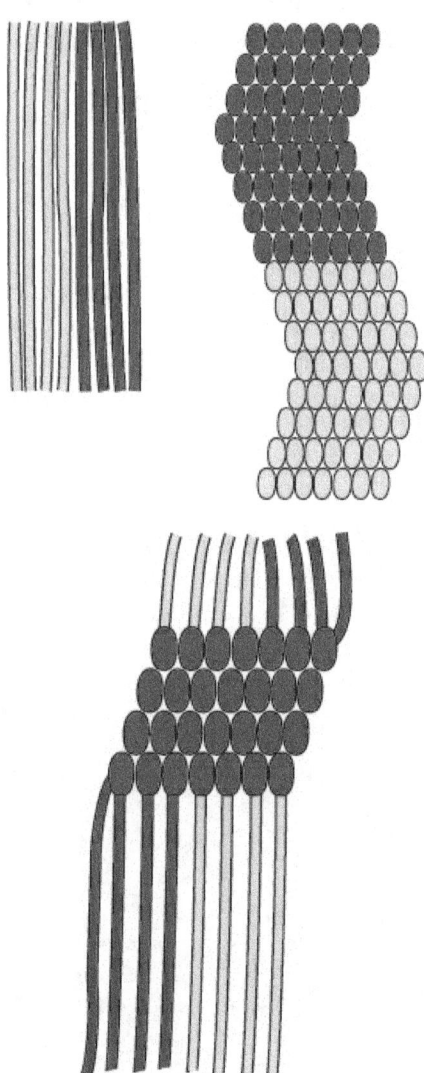

1 To begin, tie four rows of backward knots across the bracelet using the four right strands. You will see the rows begin to slant to the left.

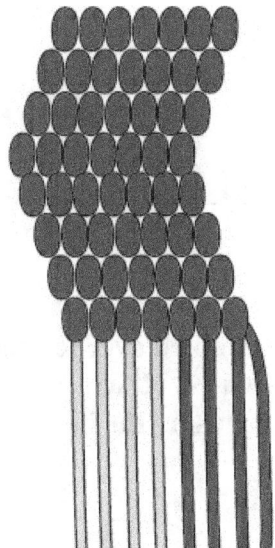

2 Tie four rows of forward knots across the bracelet using the four left strands. You will see the rows slant to the right.

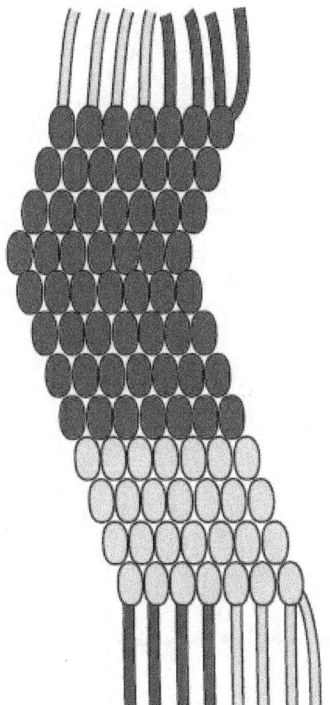

3 Tie four additional rows of forward knots across the bracelet using the four left strands. This will give you a total of eight rows that slant to the right.

4 Tie eight rows of backward knots across the bracelet. Then, tie eight rows of forward knots. Repeat until you reach the desired length.

SYMMETRICAL CHEVRONS

Start with four 72" (183cm) strands doubled over for eight strands total. Tie the strands together using an overhand knot with a ½" (1.5cm) loop at the top. Arrange the strands so the colors form a symmetrical pattern, using the illustrations below for reference. For a thicker bracelet, use more strands.

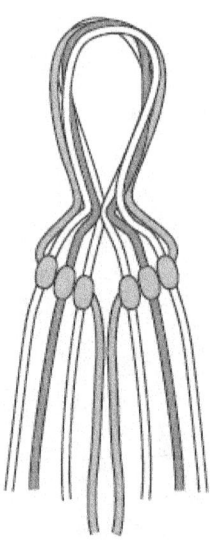

1 Using the outer left strand, tie three forward knots working toward the center of the bracelet. Then, using the outer right strand, tie three backward knots working toward the center of the bracelet.

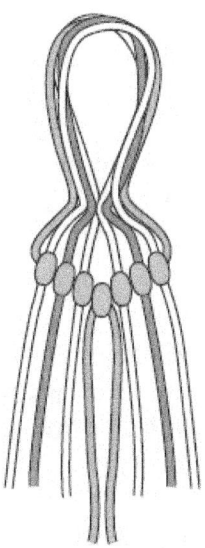

2 Tie a forward or backward knot at the center of the bracelet with the two center strands. Repeat Steps 1–2 for each row until you reach the desired length.

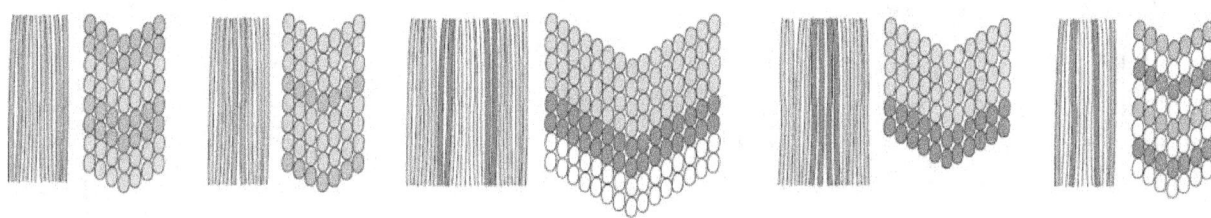

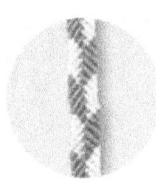

ASYMMETRICAL CHEVRONS

Start with four 72" (183cm) strands doubled over for eight strands total. Tie the strands together using an overhand knot with a ½" (1.5cm) loop at the top. Arrange the strands so the left side of the bracelet is all one color, and the right side of the bracelet is all one color, as shown in the illustrations below.

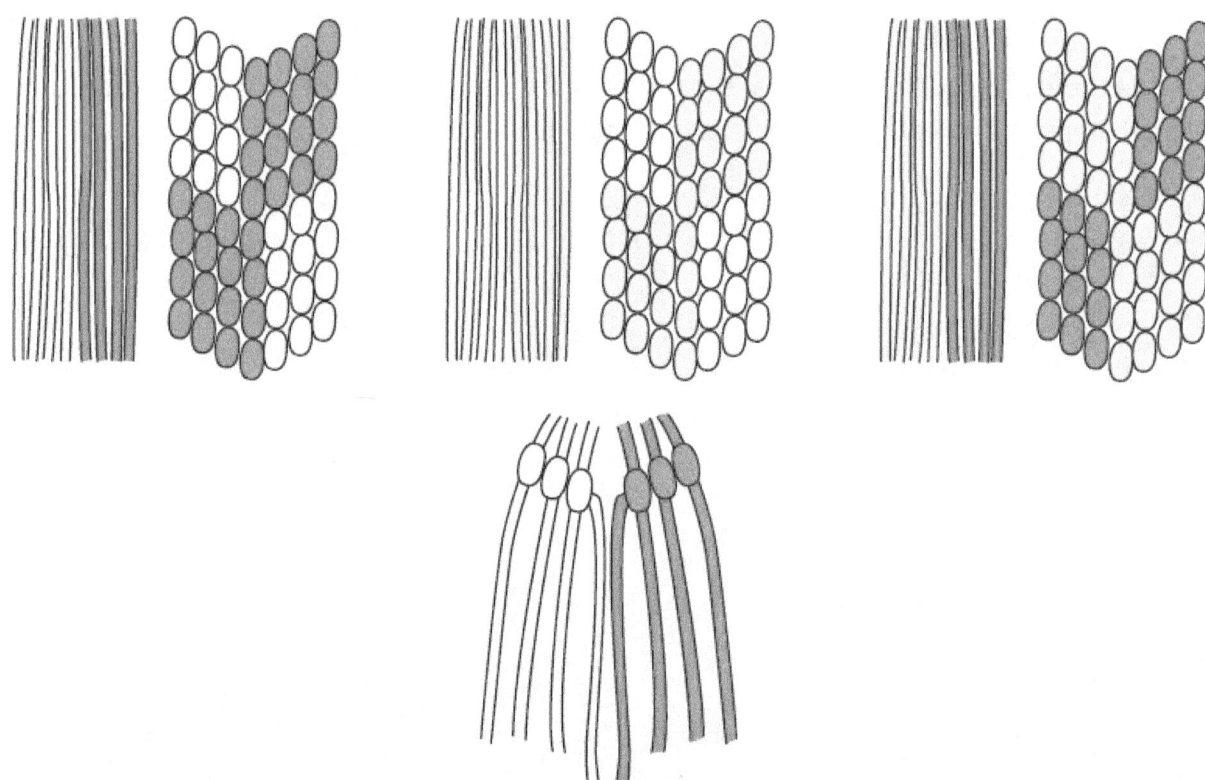

1 Using the outer left strand, tie three forward knots working toward the center of the bracelet. Then, using the outer right strand, tie three backward knots working toward the center of the bracelet.

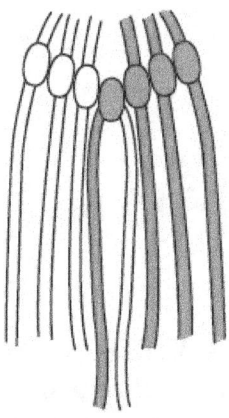

2 Tie a forward or backward knot at the center of the bracelet with the two center strands. Use the same color for the center knot for all the rows that follow. Repeat Steps 1–2 for each row until you reach the desired length.

SINGLE WAVES

Start with ten 36" (91.5cm) single strands. Tie the strands together using an overhand knot with a ½" (1.5cm) loop at the top. Position the strand colors as shown in the illustration below. Note that the two outer strands on the left side are the base strands on which all your knots will be tied.

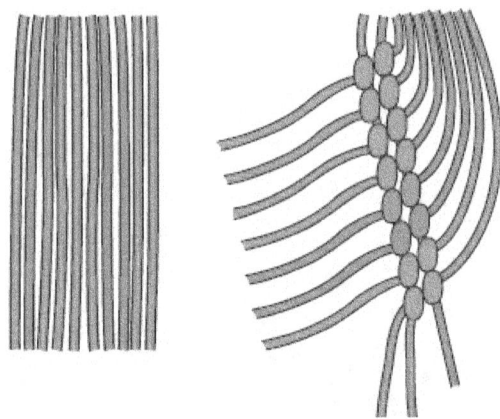

1 Using the strand that is third from the left, tie a backward knot on the base strand immediately to the left of it. Tie another backward knot on the outer base strand. Repeat, tying each of the remaining seven strands onto the base strands using backward knots. Make the last knot you tie a backward-forward knot.

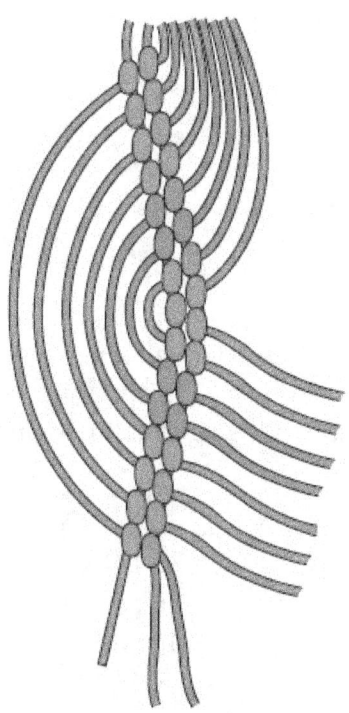

2 To reverse the direction of the wave, use the bottom working strand to tie a forward knot on the outer right base strand only. Use each of the remaining strands to tie a forward knot on each of the base strands. Make the last knot you tie a forward-backward knot. Repeat Steps 1–2 until you reach the desired length.

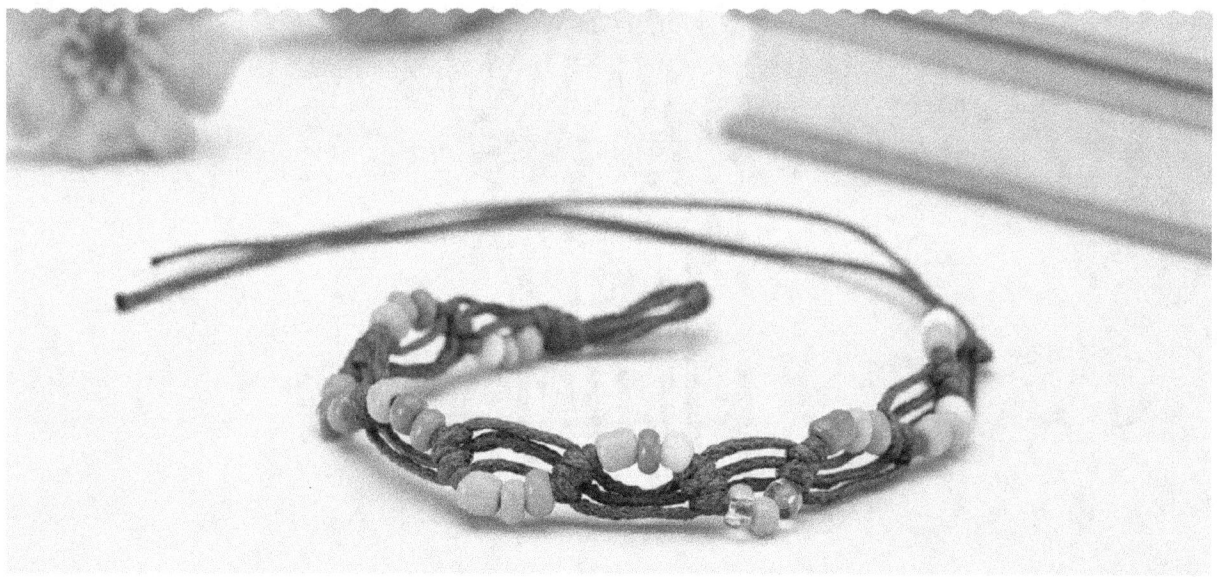

DOUBLE WAVES

Start with six 72" (183cm) strands doubled over for twelve strands total. Tie the strands together using an overhand knot with a ½" (1.5cm) loop at the top. Arrange the strands so the colors form a symmetrical pattern, using the illustration at right for reference.

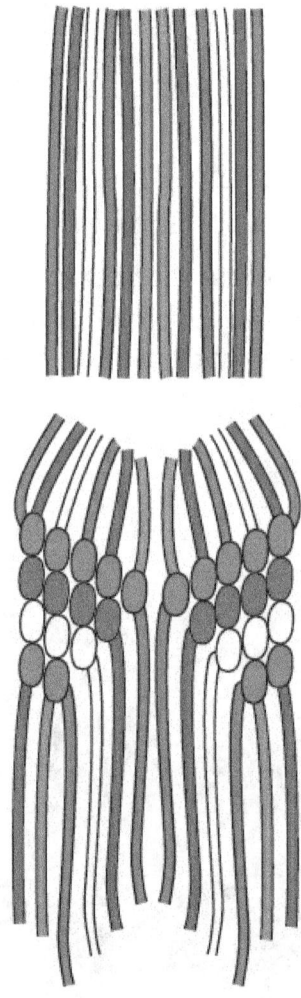

1 To begin, use the outer strands to tie knots working from each side of the bracelet toward the center. Tie five knots on each side for the first row, four knots on each side for the second row, then three knots, and then two.

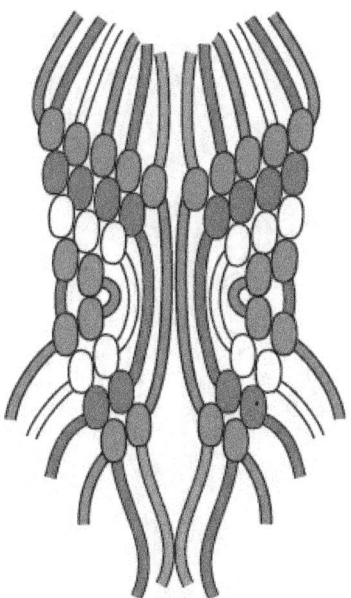

2 Starting with the third strand from the left, tie two backward knots working toward the outside of the bracelet. Repeat with the remaining three strands on the left side. Do the same on the right side of the bracelet, tying two forward knots for four rows on the right side.

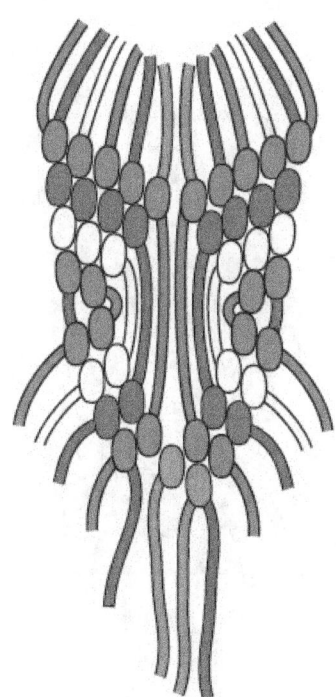

3 Tie a forward or backward knot with the two center strands. Using the right center strand, tie a forward-backward knot on the strand immediately to the right of it.

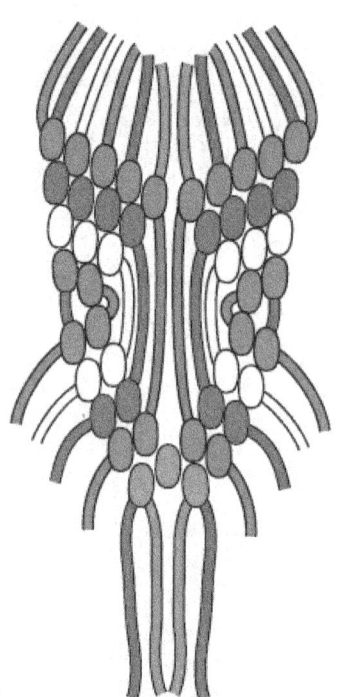

4 Using the left center strand, tie a backward-forward knot on the strand immediately to the left of it.

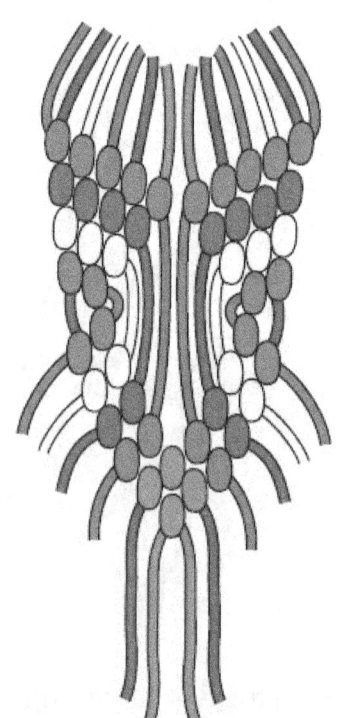

5 Tie a forward or backward knot with the two center strands.

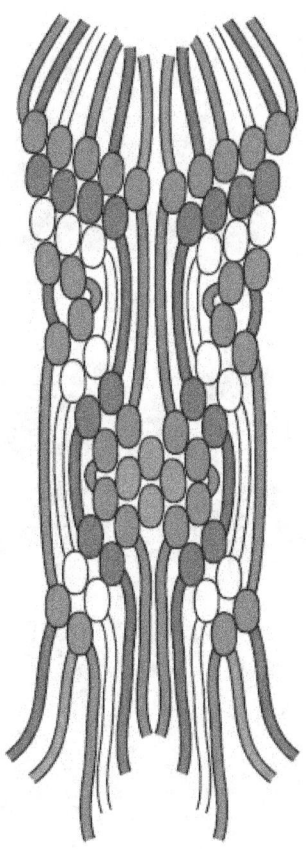

6 Starting with the fourth strand from the left, tie two forward knots, working toward the center of the bracelet. Repeat with the remaining three strands on the left side. Do the same on the right side of the bracelet, tying two backward knots for four rows on the right side.

7 Repeat Steps 2–6 until you reach the desired length.

DUAL DOUBLE WAVES

Start with ten 72" (183cm) strands doubled over for twenty strands total. Note: This design uses a lot of floss, so if you are new to making friendship bracelets, consider starting out with longer strands to ensure you don't run out! Tie the strands together using an overhand knot with a ½" (1.5cm) loop at the top. Arrange the strands so the colors form a symmetrical pattern.

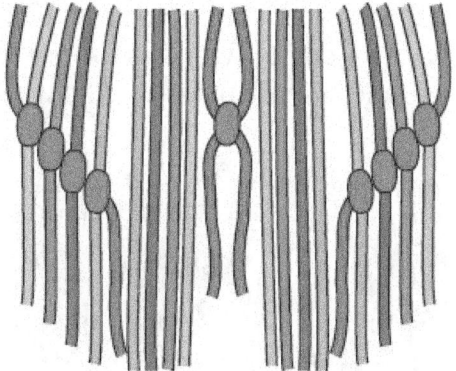

1 Tie a forward or backward knot with the two center strands. Using the outer left strand, tie four forward knots working toward the center of the bracelet. Do the same with the outer right strand, tying four backward knots working toward the center.

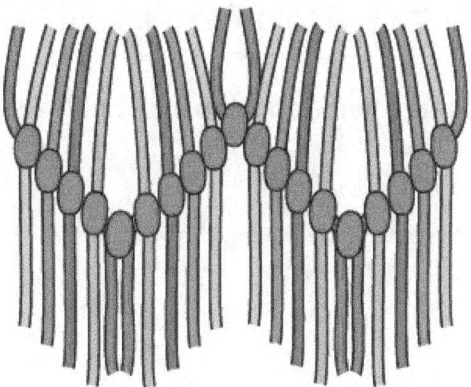

2 Using the left center strand, tie four backward knots working toward the left side of the bracelet. Do the same with the right center strand, tying four forward knots working toward the right. Tie the two strands of the same color together with a forward or backward knot where they meet on each side of the bracelet.

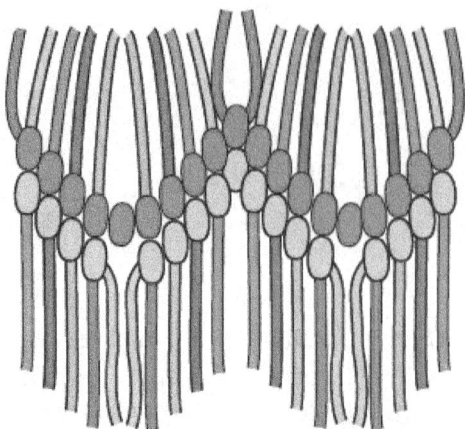

3 On the next row, tie a forward or backward knot with the two center strands. Using the outer left strand, tie four forward knots working toward the center of the bracelet. Do the same with the outer right strand, tying four backward knots working toward the center. Using the left center strand, tie four backward knots working toward the left side of the bracelet. Do the same with the right center strand, tying four forward knots working toward the right.

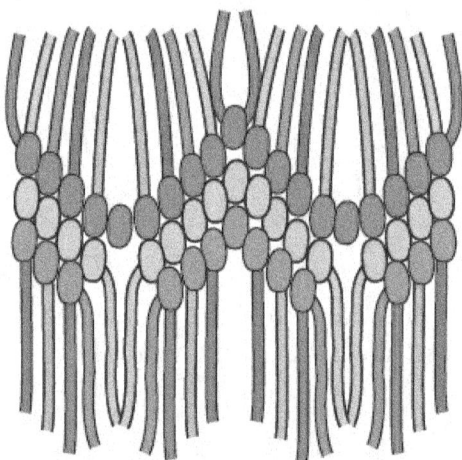

4 On the next row, repeat the pattern from Step 3, but only tie three knots for each section.

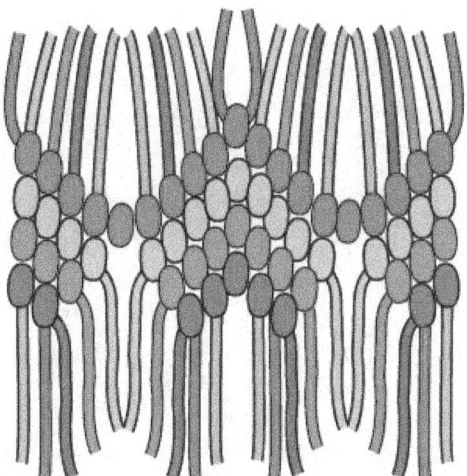

5 On the next row, repeat the pattern from Step 3, but only tie two knots for each section.

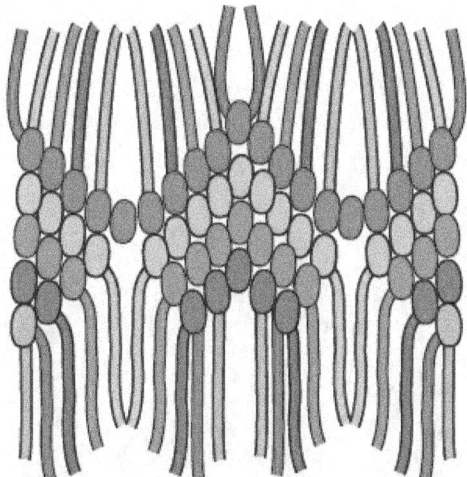

6 Using the outer left strand, tie a forward-backward knot on the strand immediately to the right of it. Do the same with the outer right strand, tying a backward-forward knot on the strand immediately to the left of it.

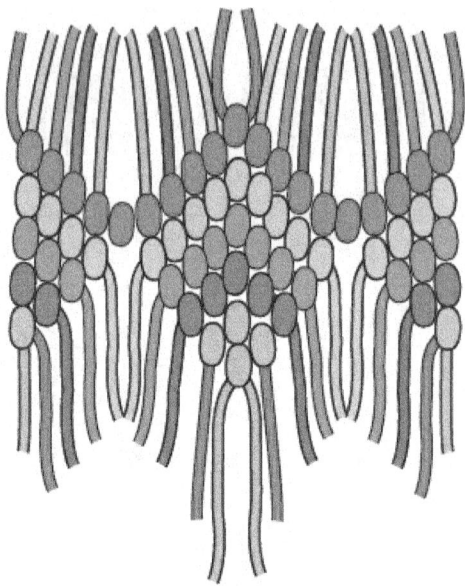

7 Tie a forward or backward knot with the two center strands. Use the right center strand to tie a forward-backward knot on the strand immediately to the right of it. Use the left center strand to tie a backward-forward knot on the strand immediately to the left of it. Tie a forward or backward knot with the two center strands.

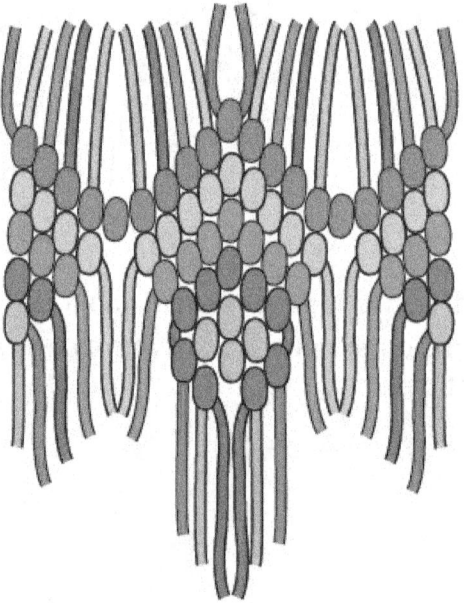

8 Starting with the eighth strand from the left side, tie two forward knots working toward the center of the bracelet. Do the same on the right side of the bracelet, tying two backward knots working toward the center.

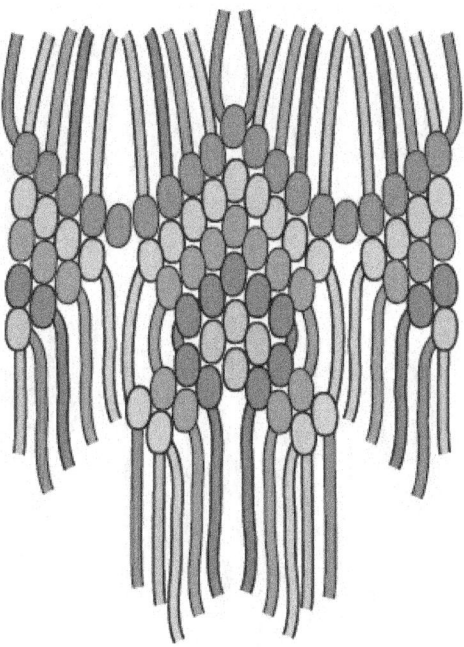

9 Repeat the pattern from Step 8 with the seventh strand from each side, tying two knots. Then, repeat the pattern with the sixth strand from each side, tying two knots.

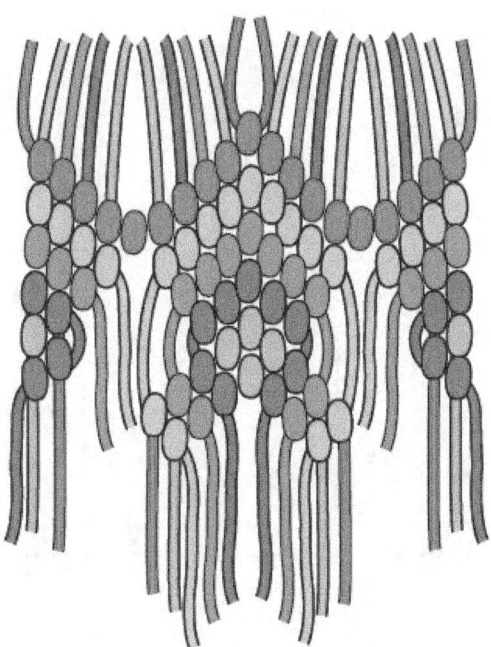

10 Starting with the third strand from the left side, tie two backward knots, working toward the outside of the bracelet. Do the same on the right side of the bracelet, tying two forward knots working toward the outside.

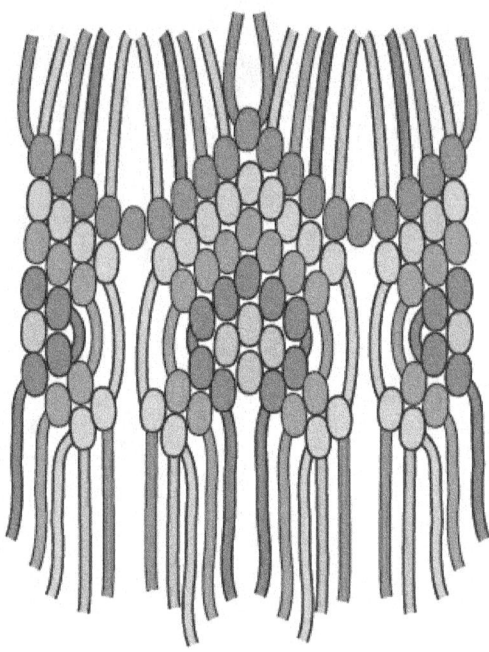

11 Repeat the pattern from Step 10 with the fourth strand from each side, tying two knots. Then, repeat the pattern with the fifth strand from each side, tying two knots.

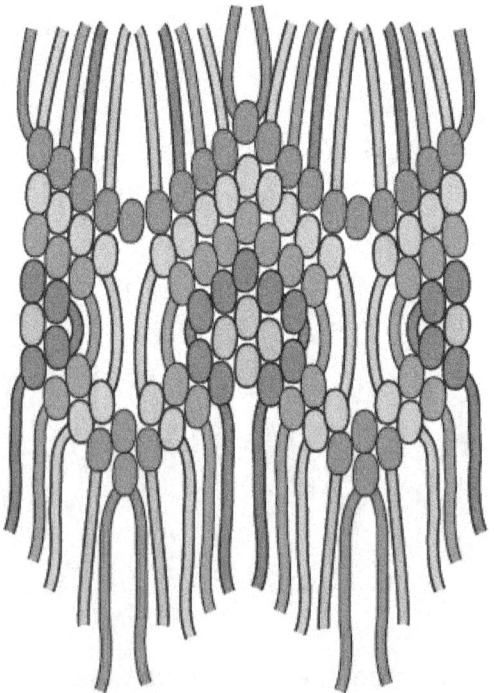

12 Repeat Step 7 using the fifth and sixth strands from the left side and the fifth and sixth strands from the right side. Continue the pattern until you reach the desired length.

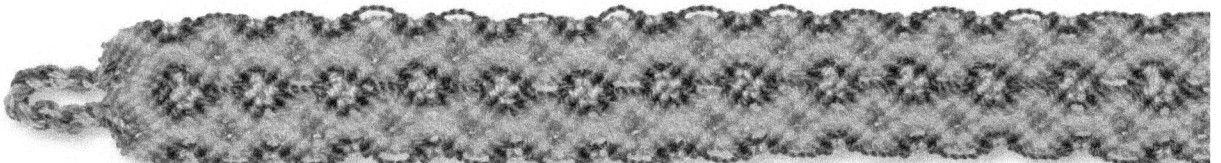

SMALL DIAMONDS

Start with three 72" (183cm) strands doubled over for six strands total. Tie the strands together using an overhand knot with a ½" (1.5cm) loop at the top. Arrange the strands so the colors form a symmetrical pattern, using the illustration at the right for reference.

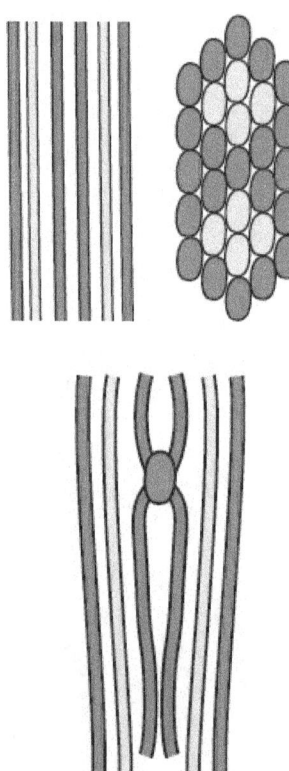

1 Tie a forward or backward knot with the two center strands.

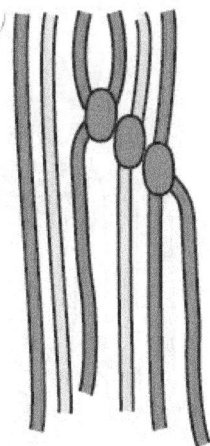

2 Using the right center strand, tie two forward knots working toward the outside of the bracelet.

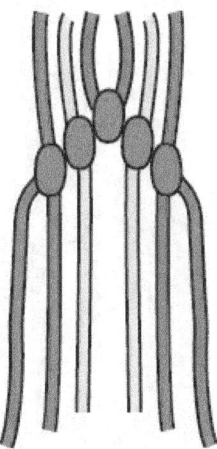

3 Using the left center strand, tie two backward knots working toward the outside of the bracelet.

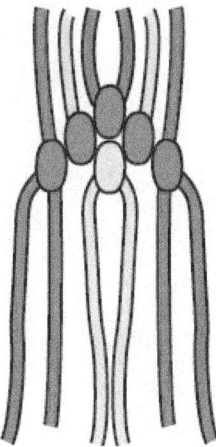

4 Tie a forward or backward knot with the two center strands.

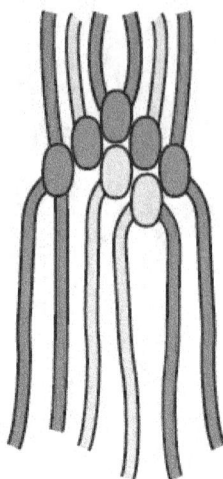

5 Using the right center strand, tie a forward-backward knot on the strand immediately to the right of it.

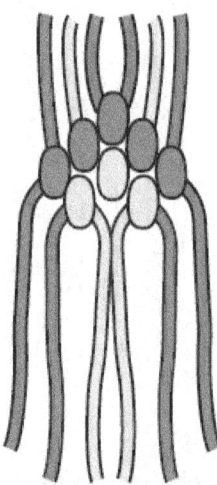

6 Using the left center strand, tie a backward-forward knot on the strand immediately to the left of it.

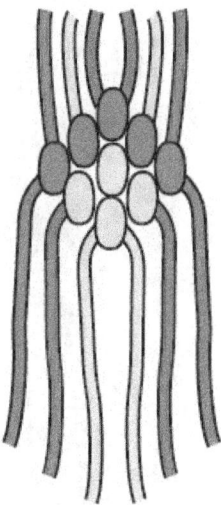

7 Tie a forward or backward knot with the two center strands.

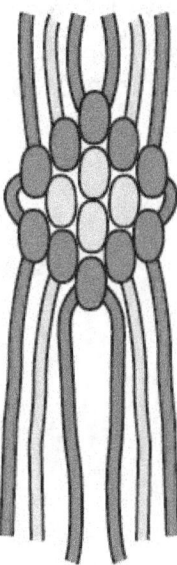

8 Using the outer left strand, tie two forward knots working toward the center of the bracelet. Do the same with the outer right strand, tying two backward knots working toward the center. Tie a forward or backward knot with the two center strands.

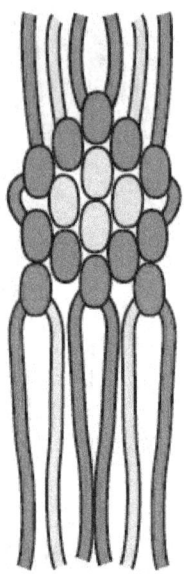

9 Using the outer left strand, tie a forward-backward knot on the strand immediately to the right of it. Do the same with the outer right strand, tying a backward-forward knot on the strand immediately to the left of it. Repeat from Step 2 until you reach the desired length.

ALTERNATING COLOR DIAMONDS

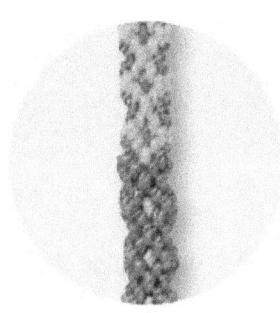

Start with three 72" (183cm) strands doubled over for six strands total. Tie the strands together using an overhand knot with a ½" (1.5cm) loop at the top. Arrange the strands so the colors form a symmetrical pattern, using the illustration at the right for reference.

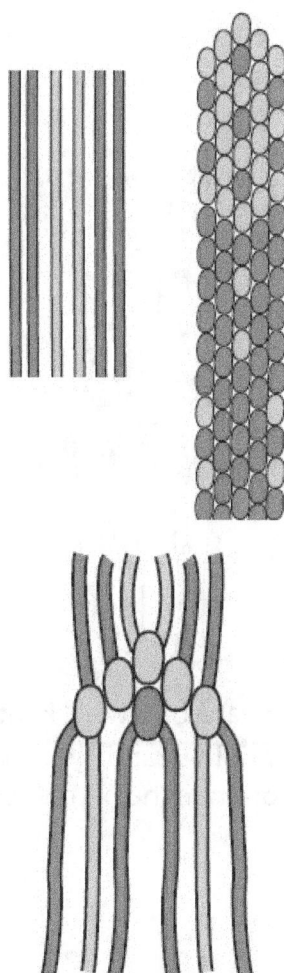

1 Tie a forward or backward knot with the two center strands. Using the right center strand, tie one forward knot and then one forward-backward knot. Repeat with the left center strand, tying one backward knot and then one backward-forward knot. Tie a forward or backward knot with the two center strands.

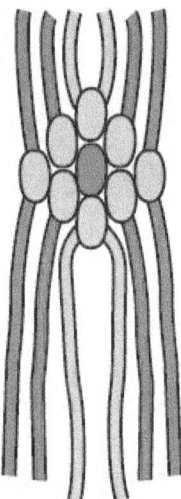

2 Using the second strand from the left, tie one forward knot. Repeat with the second strand from the right, tying one backward knot. Tie a forward or backward knot with the two center strands.

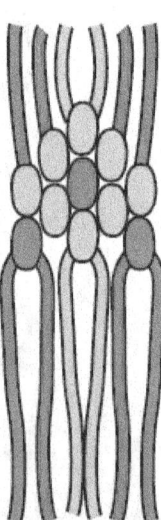

3 Using the outer left strand, tie a forward-backward knot on the strand immediately to the right of it. Do the same with the outer right strand, tying a backward-forward knot on the strand immediately to the left of it. Continue the pattern until you reach the desired length for that color section.

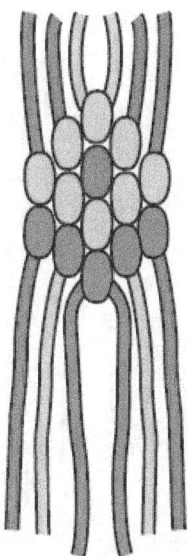

4 To change colors, use the outer left strand to tie two forward knots working toward the center of the bracelet. Do the same with the outer right strand, tying two backward knots working toward the center. Tie a forward or backward knot with the two center strands.

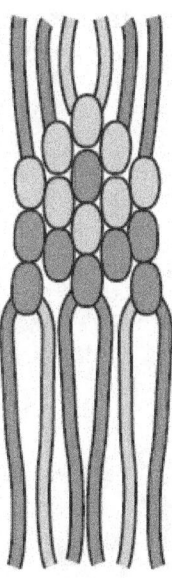

5 Using the outer left strand, tie a forward-backward knot on the strand immediately to the right of it. Do the same with the outer right strand, tying a backward-forward knot on the strand immediately to the left of it.

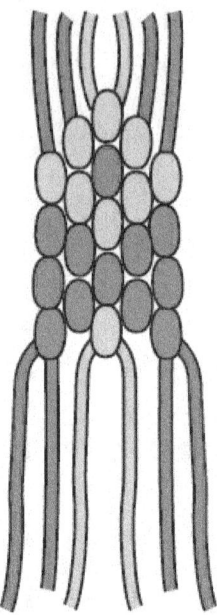

6 Using the right center strand, tie a forward knot and a forward-backward knot. Do the same with the left center strand, tying a backward knot and a backward-forward knot. Tie a forward or backward knot with the two center strands. Continue the pattern until you reach the desired length.

WIDE ALTERNATING COLOR DIAMONDS

Start with six 72" (183cm) strands doubled over for twelve strands total. Tie the strands together using an overhand knot with a ½" (1.5cm) loop at the top. Arrange the strands so the colors form a symmetrical pattern, using the illustration at the right for reference.

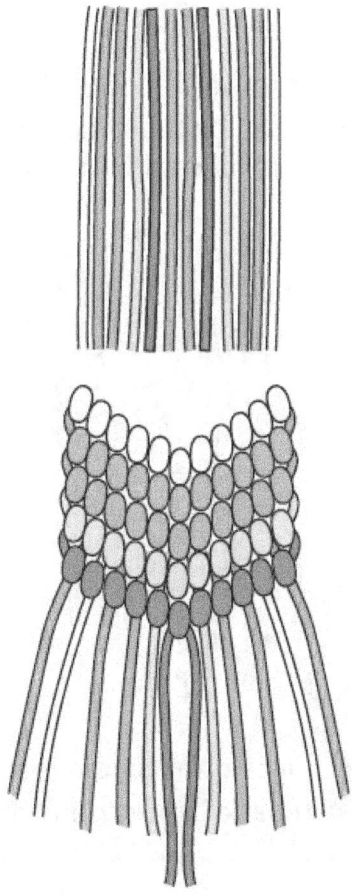

1 Using the outer left strand, tie five forward knots working toward the center of the bracelet. Do the same with the outer right strand, tying five backward knots working toward the center. Tie a forward or backward knot with the two center strands. Repeat this pattern for the next four rows.

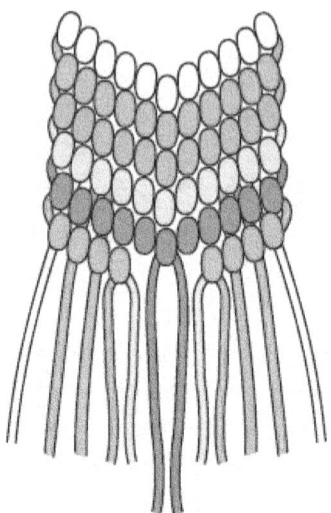

2 Using the outer left strand, tie three forward knots and one forward-backward knot working toward the center of the bracelet. Do the same with the outer right strand, tying three backward knots and one backward-forward knot working toward the center.

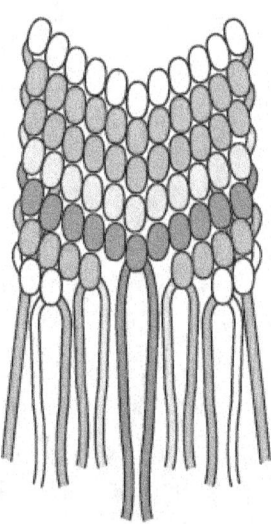

3 Repeat the pattern from Step 2 to tie two knots from each side on the next row. Make the second knot on the left side a forward-backward knot and the second knot on the right side a backward-forward knot.

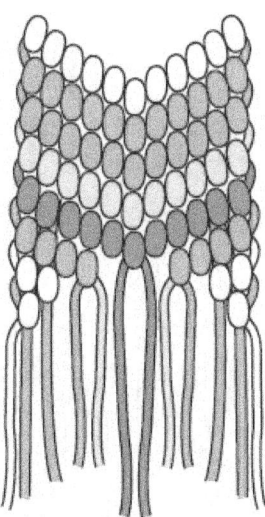

4 Using the second strand from the left side, tie a backward knot on the outer left strand. Do the same with the second strand from the right, tying a forward knot on the outer right strand.

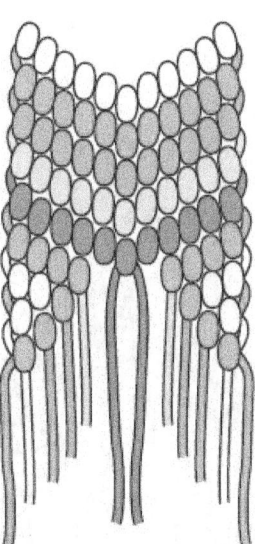

5 Using the fourth strand from the left side, tie a row of backward knots, working toward the outside of the bracelet. Do the same with the fourth strand from the right side, tying a row of forward knots working toward the outside.

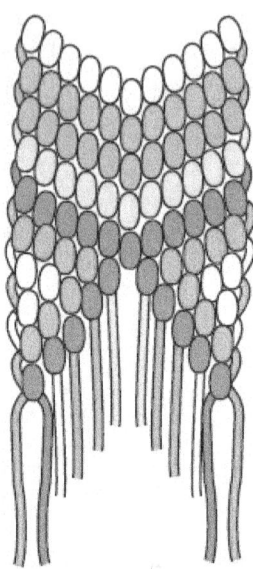

6 Repeat the pattern from Step 5 using the left and right center strands, but make the last knot on the left side a backward-forward knot and the last knot on the right side a forward-backward knot.

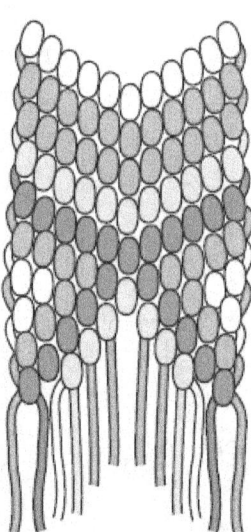

7 Tie a forward or backward knot with the center strands. Then, use the right center strand to tie two forward knots and one forward-backward knot working toward the outside. Do the same with the left center strand, tying two backward knots and one backward-forward knot working toward the outside.

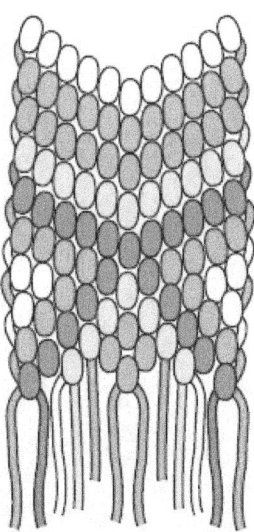

8 Tie a forward or backward knot with the center strands. Use the right center strand to tie a forward-backward knot on the strand immediately to the right of it. Use the left center strand to tie a backward-forward knot on the strand immediately to the left of it. Tie a forward or backward knot with the center strands.

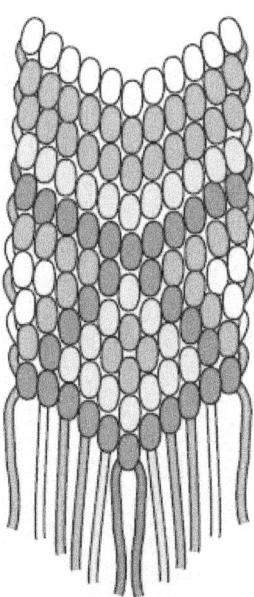

9 Using the fourth strand from the left, tie two forward knots working toward the center of the bracelet. Do the same with the fourth strand from the right, tying two backward knots working toward the center. Tie a forward or backward knot with the center strands. Repeat the pattern using the second strand from the left and right side, tying four knots for each side, and then knotting the center strands.

10 Repeat Steps 2–9 until you reach the desired length. To change colors, repeat Step 1, but only work four rows instead of five.

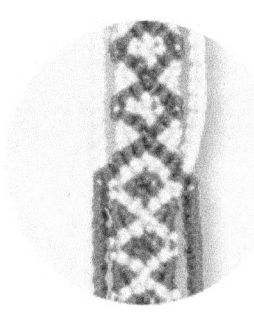

DIAMONDS IN DIAMONDS

Start with six 72" (183cm) strands doubled over for twelve strands total. Tie the strands together using an overhand knot with a ½" (1.5cm) loop at the top. Arrange the strands as shown in the illustration at the right.

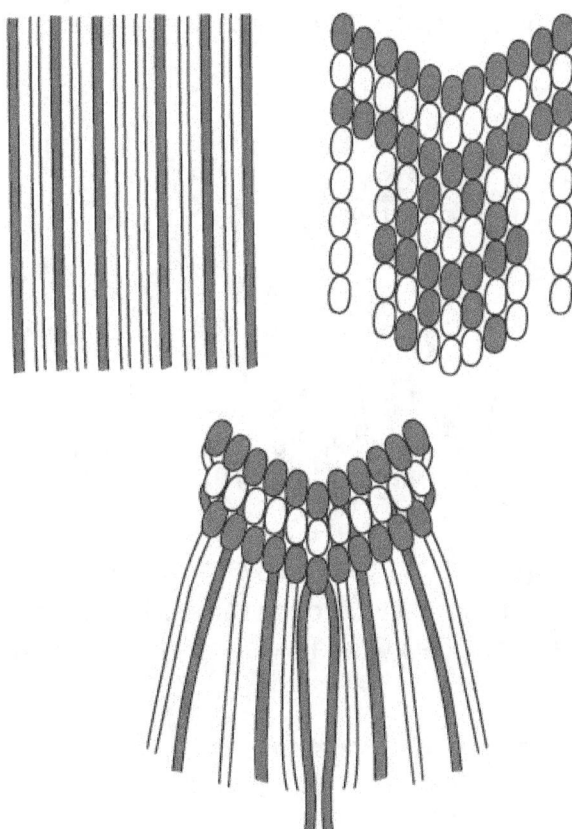

1 Using the outer left strand, tie five forward knots working toward the center of the bracelet. Do the same with the outer right strand, tying five backward knots working toward the center. Tie a forward or backward knot with the two center strands. Repeat this pattern for the next two rows.

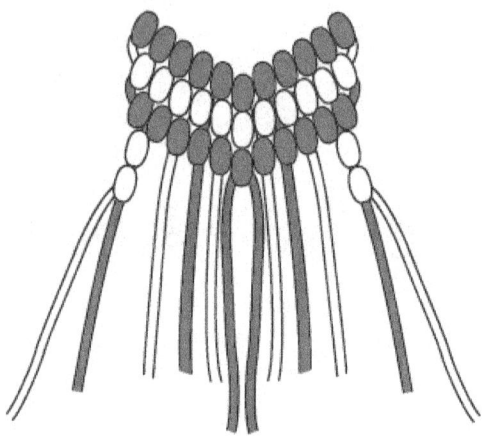

2 Use the outer left strand to begin tying forward-backward knots on the cord immediately to the right of it. Do the same with the outer right strand, tying backward-forward knots on the cord immediately to the left of it. Repeat these knots the length of a section of diamonds (note that here, for simplicity, only two of these knots are illustrated on each side).

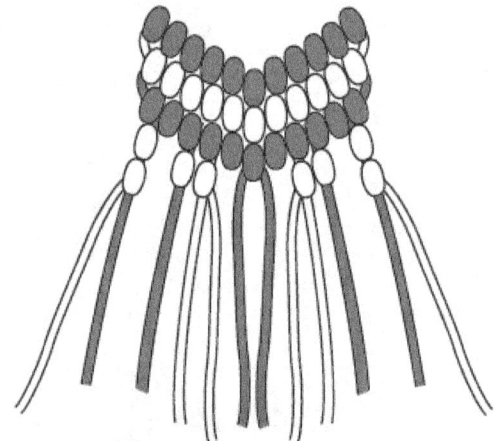

3 Using the third strand from the left, tie one forward knot and one forward-backward knot working toward the center of the bracelet. Do the same with the third strand from the right, tying one backward knot and one backward-forward knot working toward the center.

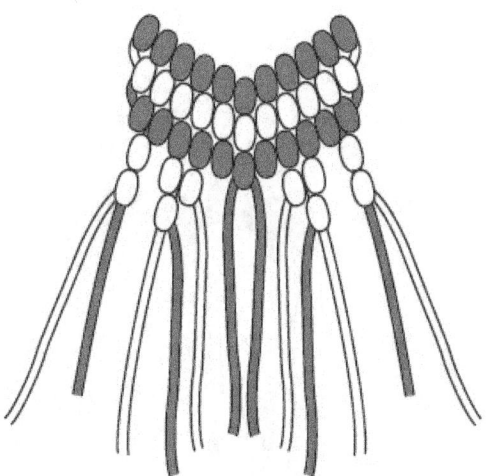

4 Using the fourth strand from the left, tie a backward knot on the strand immediately to the left of it. Repeat with the fourth knot from the right, tying a forward knot on the strand immediately to the right of it.

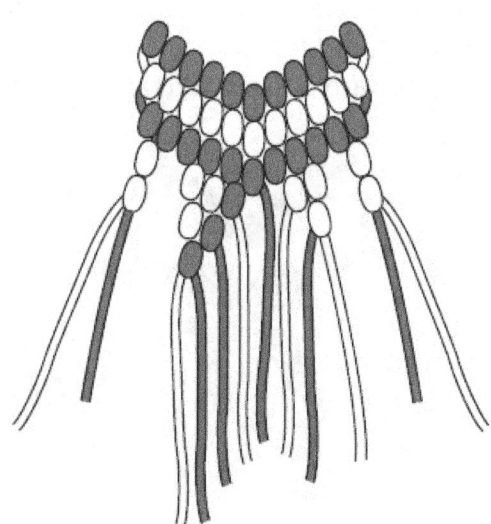

5 Using the left center strand, tie two backward knots and one backward-forward knot working toward the left side of the bracelet.

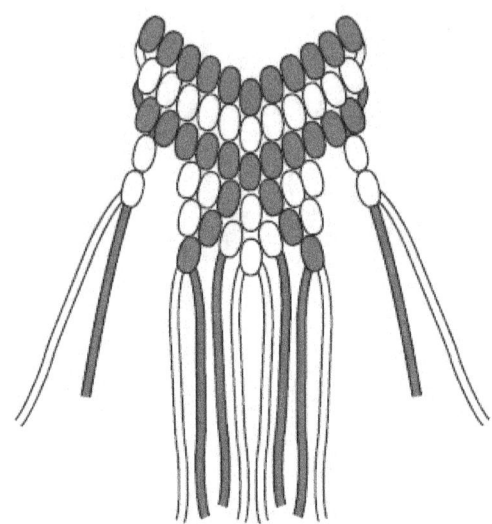

6 Using the right center strand, tie two forward knots and one forward-backward knot working toward the right side of the bracelet. Tie a forward or backward knot with the center strands. Use the right center strand to tie a forward-backward knot on the strand immediately to the right of it. Use the left center strand to tie a backward-forward knot on the strand immediately to the left of it. Tie a forward or backward knot with the center strands.

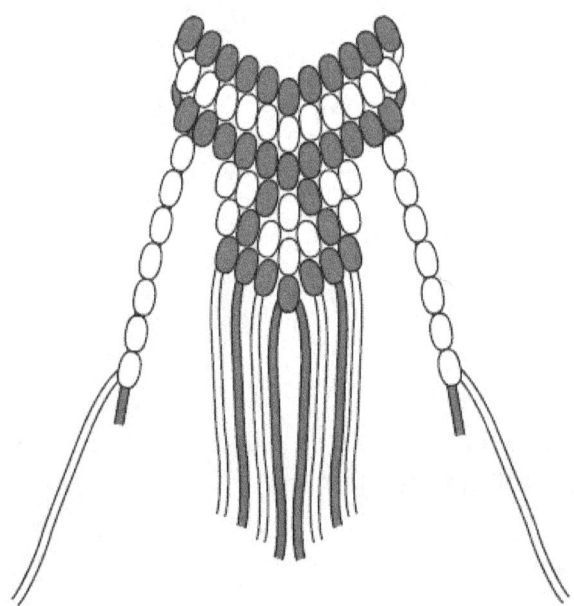

7 Using the fourth strand from the left, tie two forward knots working toward the center of the bracelet. Repeat with the fourth strand from the right, tying two backward knots working toward the center. Tie a forward or backward knot with the center strands.

8 Repeat Steps 3–7 for each diamond. To change colors, tie a row of chevron stripes (see this page) using the outer left and right strands.

HEMP DESIGNS

Hemp is a wonderful material to use for creating bracelets and other jewelry designs. It is natural, durable, and holds its shape incredibly well. It's perfect for first-time knotters, as knots made in hemp are easy to follow, so correcting mistakes is simple. Don't let color keep you from trying this wonderful material. Hemp is available in its natural tan, as well as a variety of other bright, variegated, and metallic colors, so you will be sure to find something that fits your particular taste and style. Hemp jewelry makes a wonderful addition to casual outfits, or can be dressed up with complex knots or beading to create one-of-a-kind pieces that you'll love to wear for a night out. Check out the different projects shown here, and all the ideas for customizing them to make them your very own!

THE BASICS

Hemp comes in a variety of colors and a variety of thicknesses. If you want to create a thick chunky project, use thick hemp. If you'd like to incorporate beads in your design, select thin hemp that will fit through the holes in your beads.

Measuring

Hemp projects are typically made up of working strands, which are used to tie the knots, and center strands, around which the knots are tied. Because of this, working strands should be five to six times as long as the desired length of the finished piece if you intend to use close, dense knots, such as square knots. The more unknotted space or beads you plan to incorporate in your design, the shorter the working strands can be. If you knot tightly, you will likely use more cord, while if you knot loosely, you won't use as much. Just keep in mind, it's always better to have too much cord than too little! You can always make smaller projects like keychains from your leftovers.

For insurance, center strands should be about twice as long as the desired length of the finished piece, plus enough length to allow you to tie your ending knot easily. Again, too much is always better than too little!

Getting started

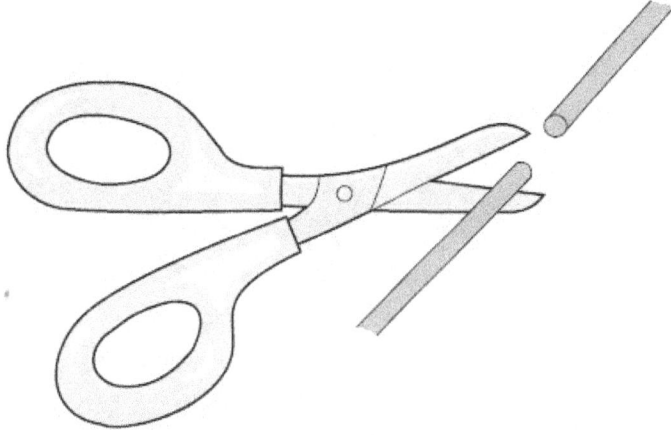

1 Measure and trim strands of hemp to the size you need.

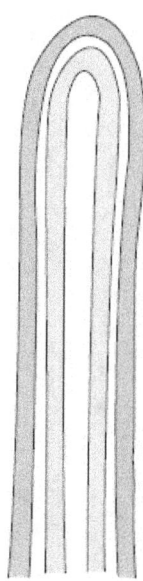

2 Fold the strands in half to find the center, and align the center points.

3 Tie an overhand knot at the folded end of the hemp to form a ½" (1.5cm) loop. Bring the working strands to the outside (left and right sides) of the piece before you begin knotting.

Tips

Adding beads. Select beads with holes large enough to fit over the hemp strands you are using. Beads are typically threaded onto both center strands, although they can be added to just one center strand, or the outer working strands. If the holes in the beads you wish to use are too small, incorporate beading wire into your design so you can thread the beads into the wire instead of the hemp (see this page).

Tightening knots. For strong knots, especially beginning and ending knots, tighten each strand individually. If possible, use pliers to pull strands tight for the ending knot.

Not enough cord. If you're running short on cord toward the end of your design, try switching the working strands with the center strands. Switching the strands will show a little, so hide the transition with a bead or in the middle of a knot if possible. Use glue as needed.

Closures

Hemp projects are simple to finish with a loop on one end and a knot on the other. For a more finished look, however, you can add jewelry closures.

To finish a project without tying knots, use ribbon crimps. Center the ends of the hemp strands on the ribbon crimp. Evenly pinch down on the crimp using pliers. Use jump rings to attach a clasp to the ribbon crimps. Be sure to twist the jumps rings open and closed so that they retain their shape. Do not pull the rings open.

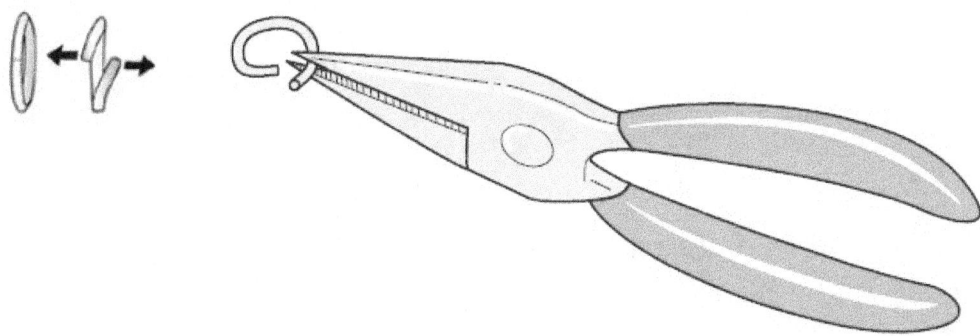

Twist your jump ring open, making sure you maintain the circular shape. Do not pull the jump ring open from side to side so that it loses its shape.

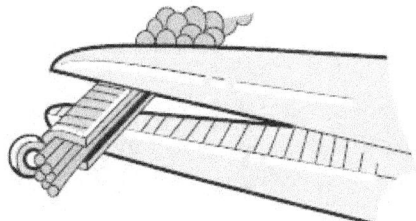

Place the ends of your design in a ribbon crimp, and squeeze the crimp closed with pliers.

Use jump rings to attach a clasp to the ribbon crimps.

OVERHAND KNOT

Simple Overhand Knot Bracelet

Start with three 24" (61cm) strands of hemp in the colors you desire. Tie the strands together using an overhand knot with a ½" (1.5cm) loop at the top. Pull the knot tight and dot with glue if desired. Use all three strands to tie overhand knots at even intervals until you reach the desired length. Finish the piece with a double overhand knot (tie one overhand knot, and then tie a second one on top of the first).

Basic overhand knot

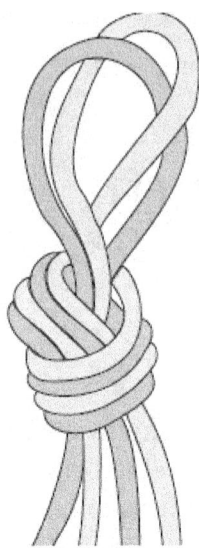

Overhand knot with loop

OVERHAND KNOT VARIATIONS

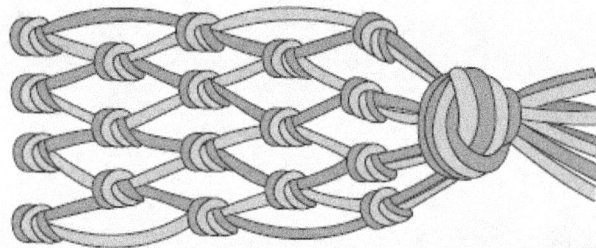

Eight-strand alternating overhand knot

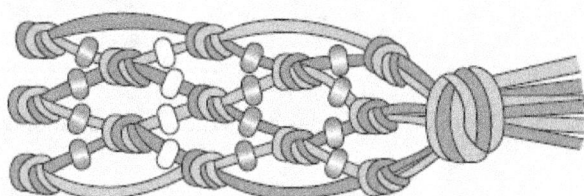

Six-strand alternating overhand knot with beads

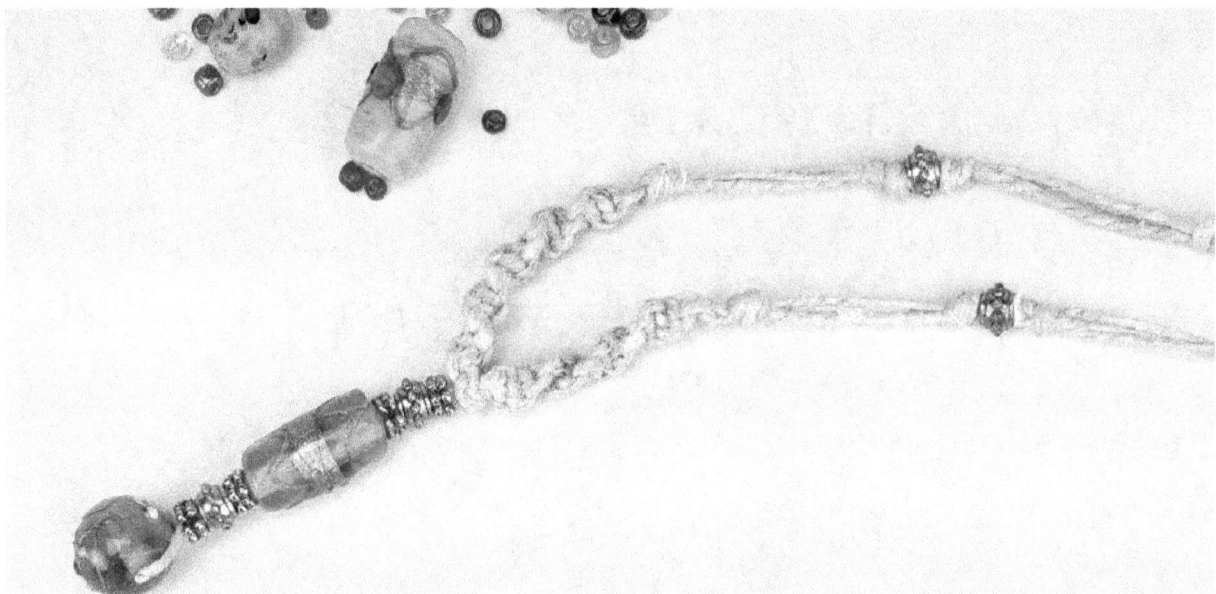
Overhand knots make for quick projects! This one incorporates beads and uses a half knot twist above the pendant.

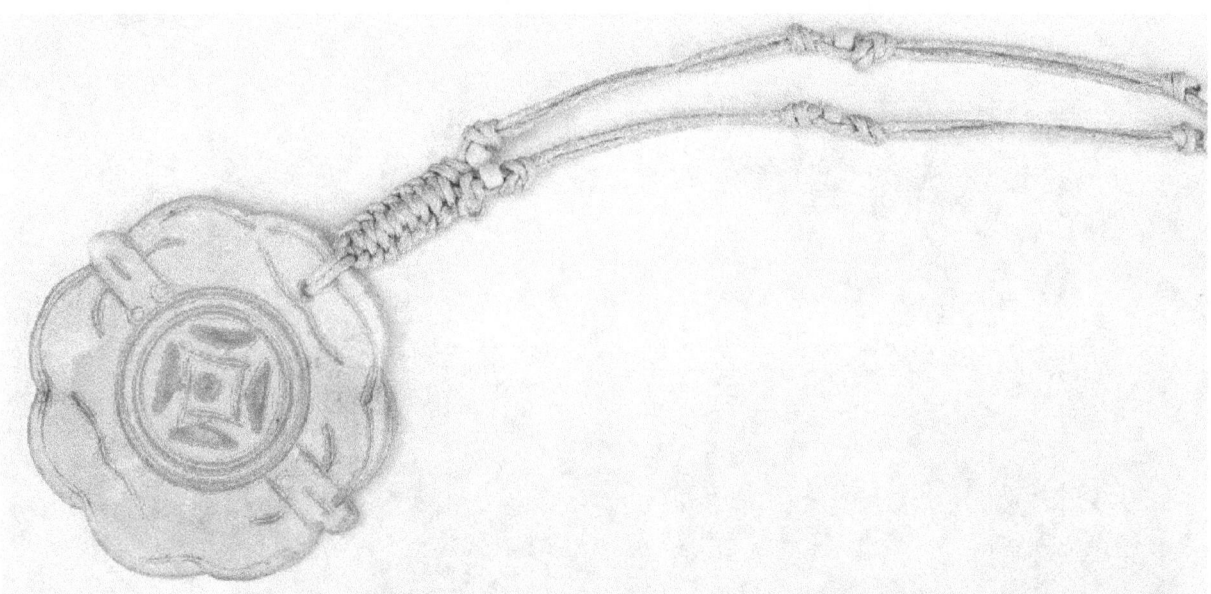
Small colored beads pop against the natural hemp in this design.

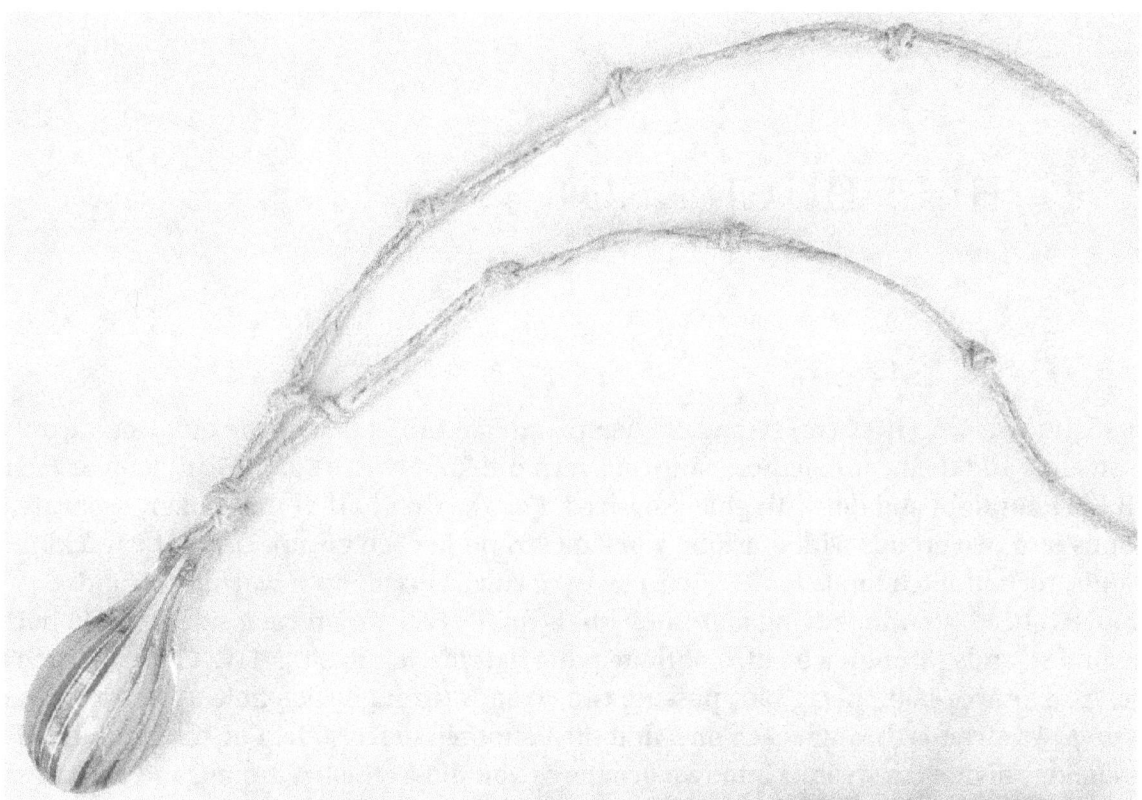
This design is simple and classic, using easy overhand knots for the necklace strands and a single pendant focal piece.

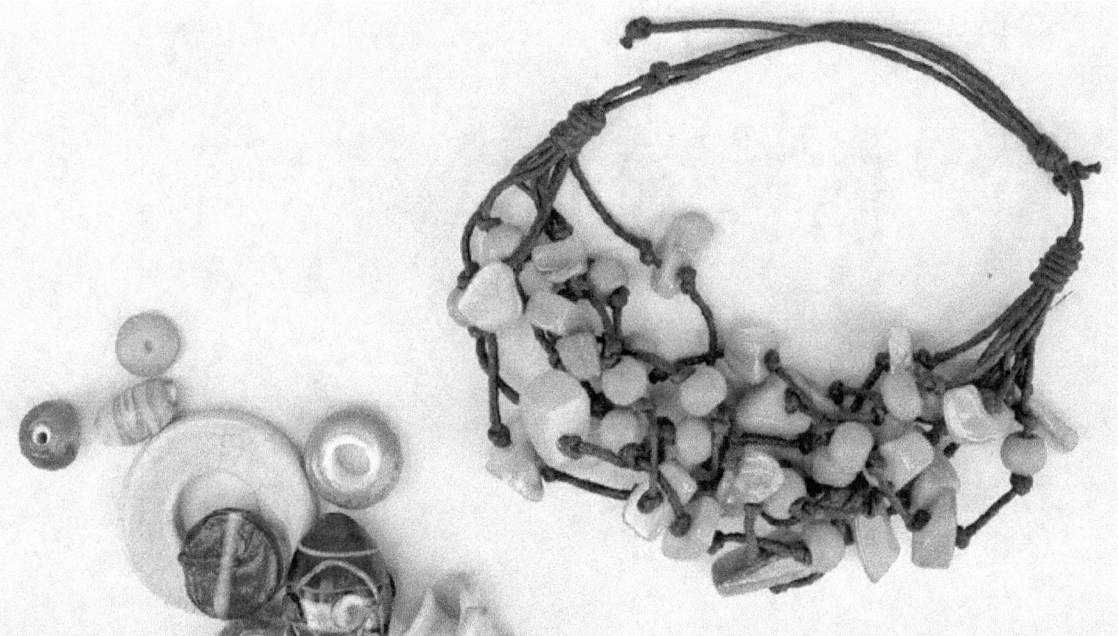
A multi-strand bracelet is easy to achieve with overhand knots. Tie your strands together. Then, add beads to each strand, tying overhand knots before and after each bead to keep it in place.

HALF HITCH KNOT

Half Hitch Choker

Start with two 40" (101.5cm) strands of hemp and one 150" (381cm) strand. Double over the strands and tie them together using an overhand knot with a ½" (1.5cm) loop at the top. Pull the knot tight and dot with glue if desired. For the first half of the choker, separate the strands into two groups with one long working strand in each group. Using the working strands, tie half hitch knots for 2" (5cm) on each side. Thread both working strands through a bead. Continue tying half hitch knots for 1" (2.5cm) on each side. Thread both working strands through a bead. Continue tying half hitch knots for 1¼" (3cm) on each side. Add a three-hole spacer bar, passing two strands through each hole. Add three beads, passing two strands through each one, and then another spacer bar. For the second half of the choker, divide the strands into two groups as you did at the beginning, and reverse the knotting pattern used for the first half. Finish with an overhand knot.

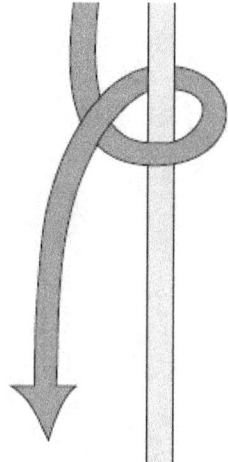

Left half hitch

Repeating left half hitch

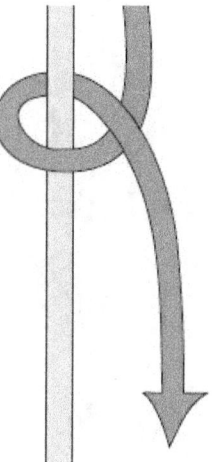

Right half hitch

HALF HITCH KNOT VARIATIONS

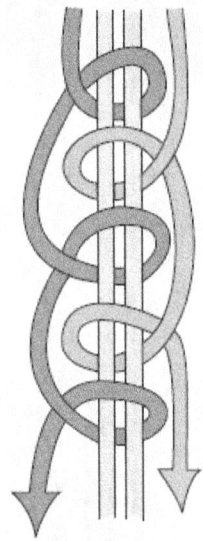

Alternating left and right half hitch knots

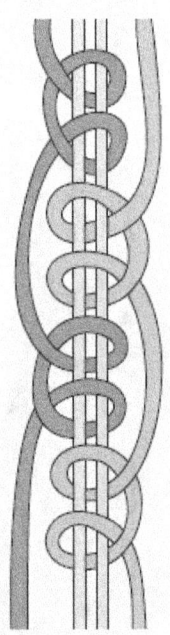

Double alternating left and right half hitch knots

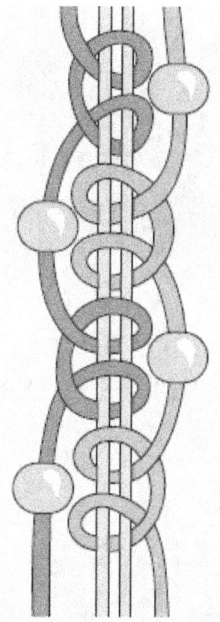

Double alternating left and right half hitch knots with beads

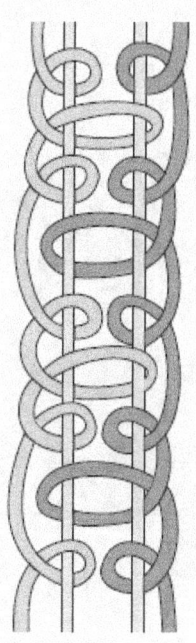

Triple alternating left and right half hitch knots (flat band)

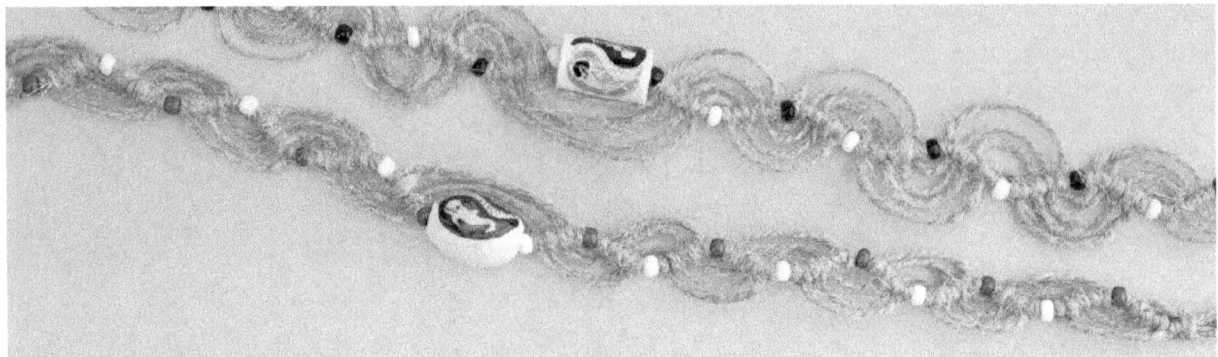
Adding beads to the base strand gives these bracelets an extra special touch.

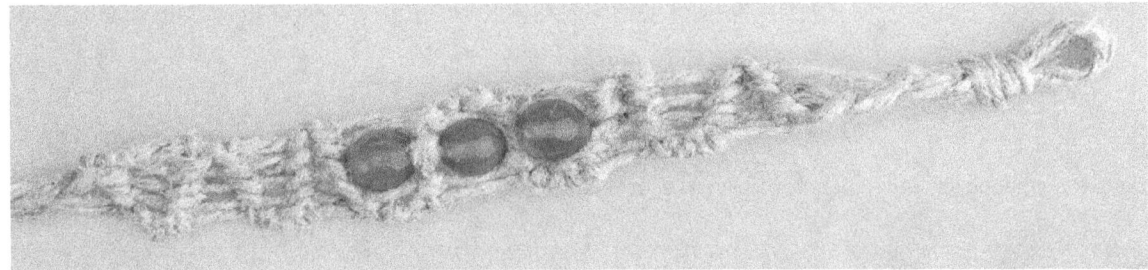
Large beads threaded onto the working strands can be used to make a focal section in a diagonal half hitch bracelet.

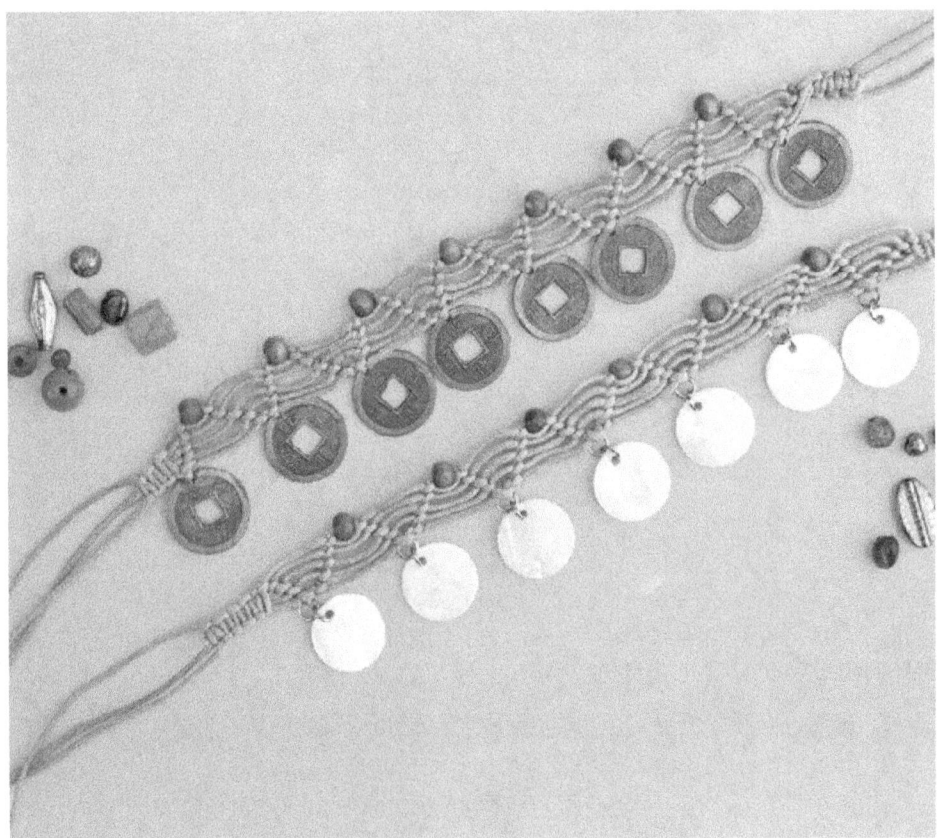
Use jump rings to add a row of large, dangling beads along the length of your bracelet.

DIAGONAL HALF HITCH

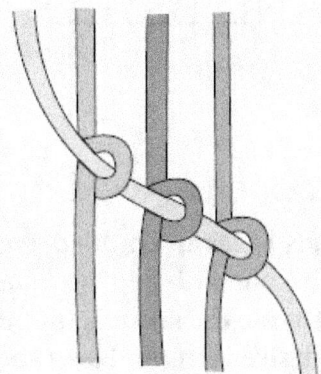

To the left

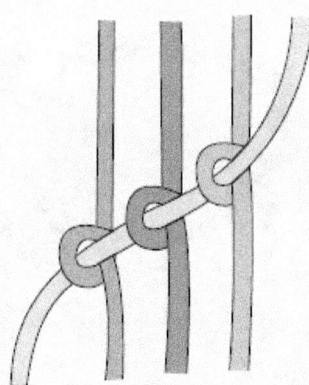

To the right

THREE-STRAND BRAID

Three-Strand Braid Bracelet or Necklace

Start with three 48" (122cm) strands of hemp doubled over for six strands total. Tie the strands together using an overhand knot with a ½" (1.5cm) loop at the top. Pull the knot tight and dot with glue if desired. Divide the strands into three groups of two and braid them together until you reach the desired length. Keep each pair of strands side by side as you work the braid. Add beads to strands at the center of the braid or at the end for a closure. Finish with an overhand knot.

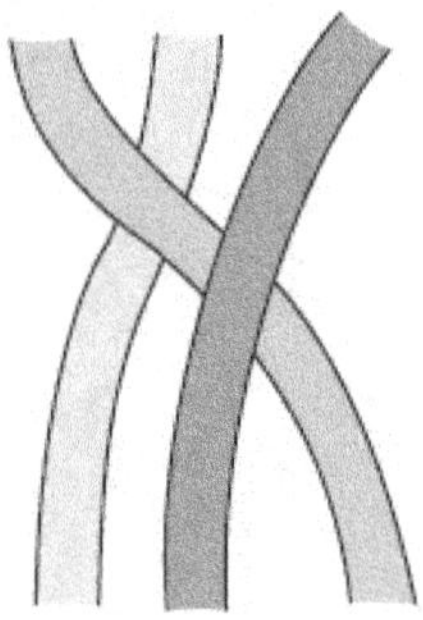

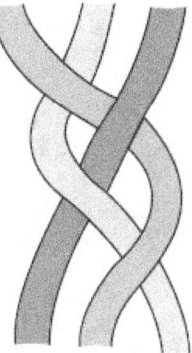

Bring the left strand over the center strand. Then, bring the right strand over the center strand. Repeat.

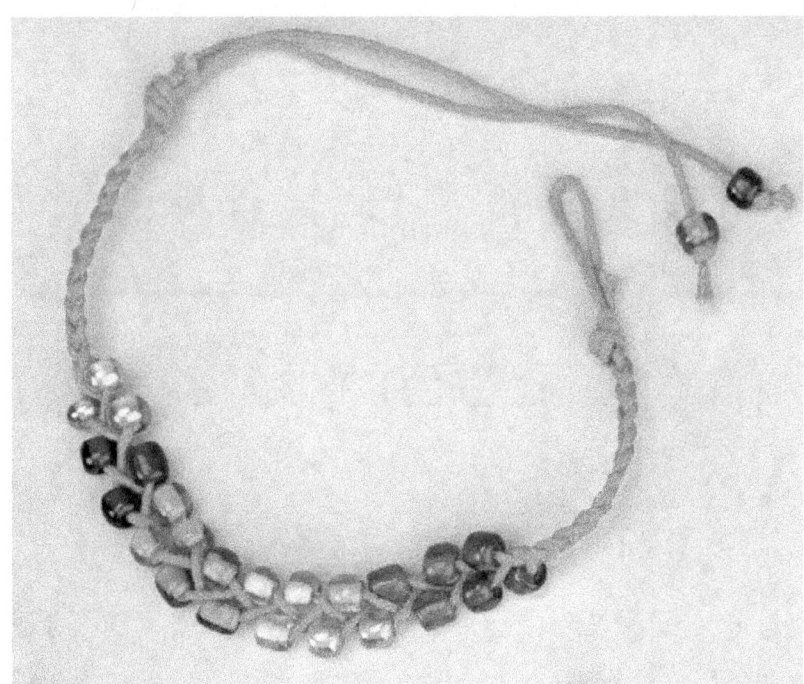

Enhance a simple braid by making a beaded focal section. Add beads to the outer strands as you braid them until the focal section reaches the length you desire.

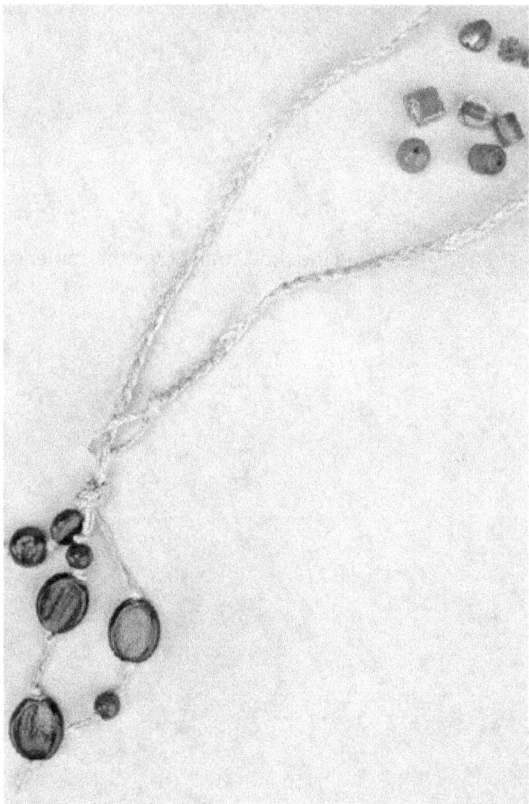

Turn your braid into a lariat necklace or belt. At one end, tie the strands together in an overhand knot. Divide the strands and add beads to each one.

Create the focal section of this necklace by tying the strands together using an overhand knot. Thread beads onto each strand. Then, tie all the strands together again at the end of the focal section.

FOUR-STRAND ROUND BRAID

Four-Strand Round Braid Bracelet

Start with four 24" (61cm) single strands of hemp or two 48" (122cm) strands doubled over for a total of four. Tie the strands together using an overhand knot with a ½" (1.5cm) loop at the top. Pull the knot tight and dot with glue if desired. Follow the illustrations to braid the strands together using a four-strand round braid until you reach the desired length. Finish with an overhand knot.

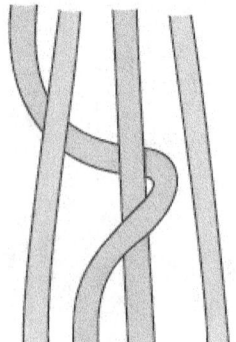

Bring the right strand under the two in the center and back over one

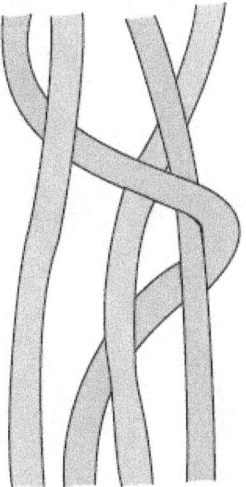

Bring the left strand under the two in the center and back over one

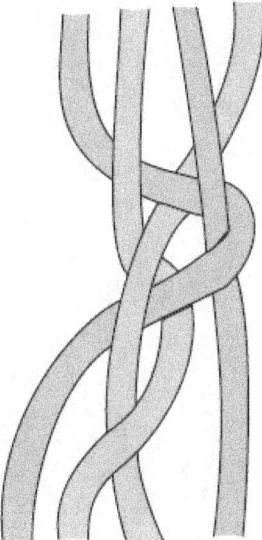

Repeat with the right strand (under two, over one)

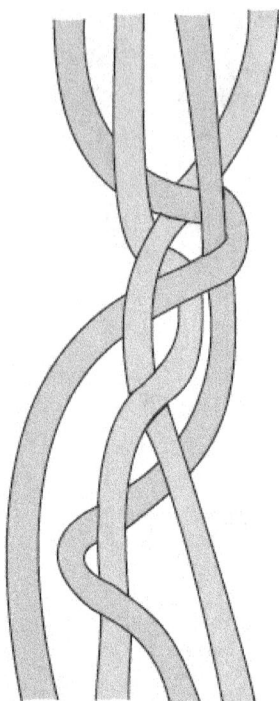

Repeat with the left strand (under two, over one)

FIVE-STRAND BRAID

Five-Strand Braid Bracelet

Start with five 24" (61cm) single strands of hemp in the colors you desire. Tie the strands together using an overhand knot with a ½" (1.5cm) loop at the top. Pull the knot tight and dot with glue if desired. Follow the illustrations to braid the strands together using a five-strand braid until you reach the desired length. Finish with an overhand knot.

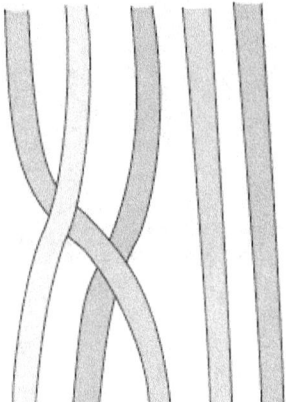

Bring the left strand under one and over one

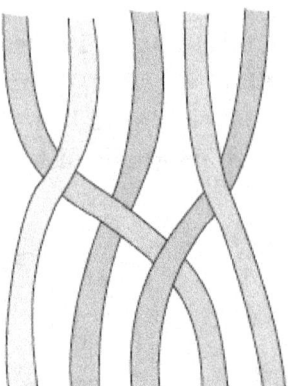

Bring the right strand under one and over one

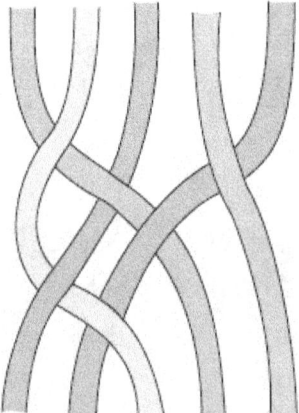

Repeat with the left strand (under one, over one)

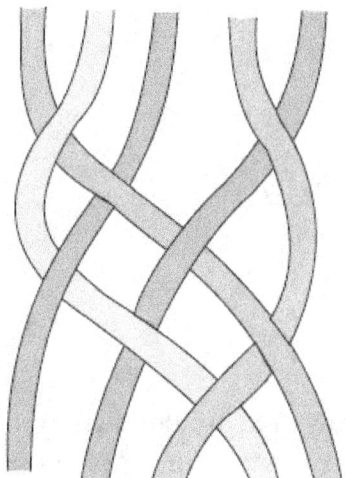

Repeat with the right strand (under one, over one)

WOVEN BANDS

Six-Strand Woven Band

Start with three 24" (61cm) strands of hemp doubled over for six filler strands total. Cut a 110" (279.5cm) strand of hemp for the weaving cord. Tie an overhand knot at one end of the weaving cord. Tie the filler strands onto the end of the weaving cord using an overhand knot with a ½" (1.5cm) loop at the top. Pull the knot tight and dot with glue if desired. Divide the filler strands into three groups of two strands each. Bring the weaving cord through the filler strands as illustrated below at the right until you reach the desired length. Add beads onto the center two filler strands at even intervals as desired. Finish with an overhand knot.

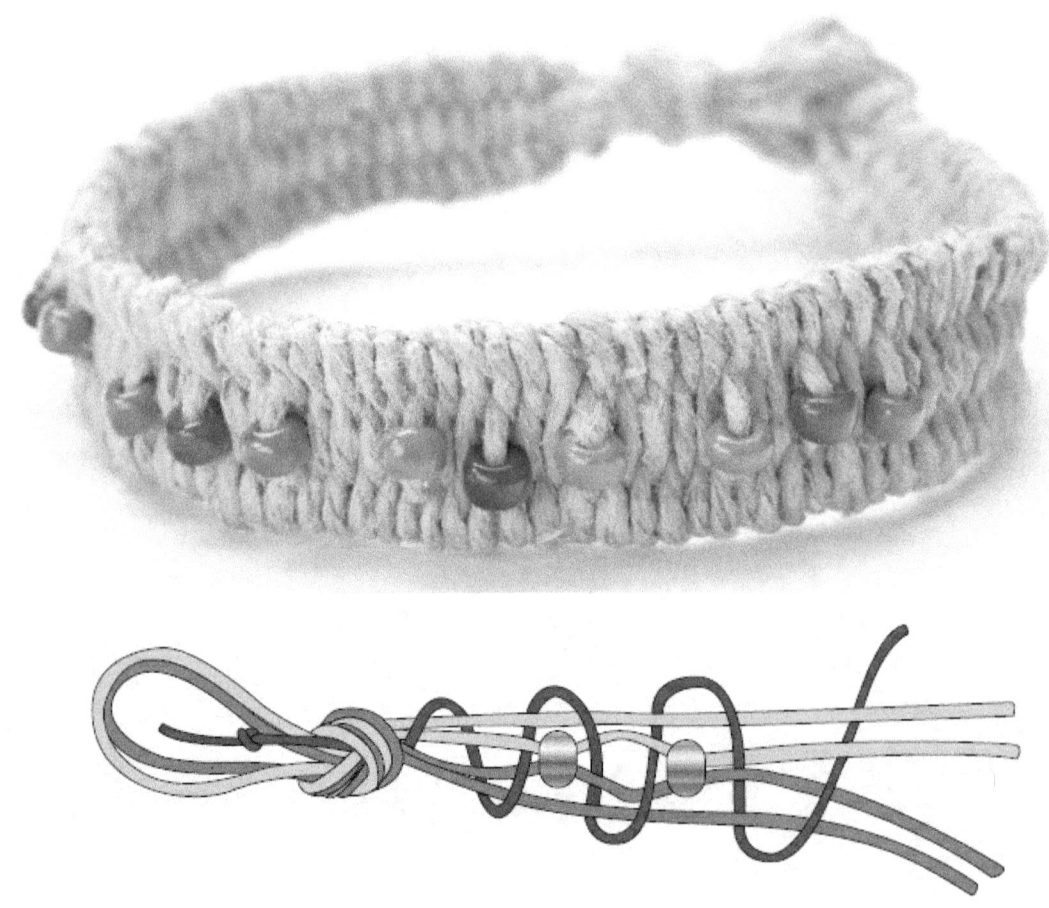

Four-strand woven band

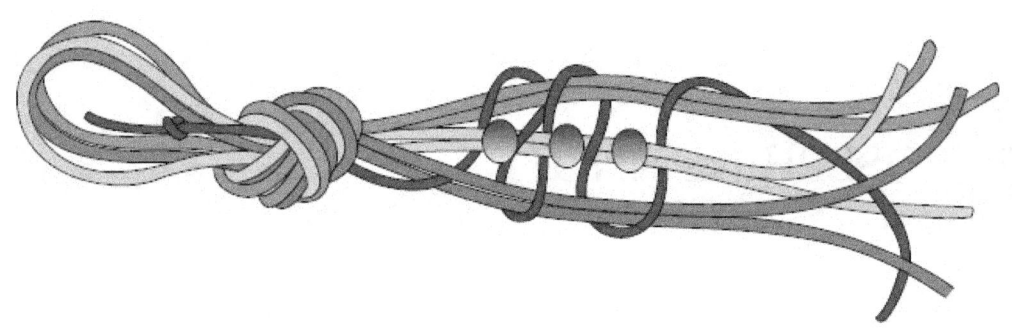

Six-strand woven band

JOSEPHINE KNOT

Josephine Knot Bracelet

Start with two 200" (508cm) strands of hemp doubled over for four strands total. Tie the strands together using an overhand knot with a ½" (1.5cm) loop at the top. Pull the knot tight and dot with glue if desired. Follow the illustrations to tie Josephine knots, treating each pair of strands as one, until you reach the desired length. Keep each pair of strands side by side as you shape the knot. You can tie the knots tightly together, or you can space them out for a more airy design. Finish with an overhand knot.

SQUARE KNOT

Square Knot Bracelet

Start with one 24" (61cm) strand and one 68" (172.5cm) strand of hemp, both doubled over for four strands total. Tie the strands together using an overhand knot with a ½" (1.5cm) loop at the top. Pull the knot tight and dot with glue if desired. Follow the illustrations to tie square knots around the short center strands with the long working strands until you reach the desired length. Thread beads onto both center strands as desired and tie square knots around them with the working strands. Finish with an overhand knot.

Bring the right working strand under the center strands and over the left working strand. Bring the left working strand over the center strands and under the right working strand.

Bring the right working strand over the center strands and under the left working strand. Bring the left working strand under the center strands and over the right working strand.

ADDING BEADS

Use beading wire in your hemp designs to add beads with holes that are too small to be threaded directly onto the hemp. Attach beading wire to a jump ring with a crimp bead or tube. Then, thread the hemp strands for your project through the jump ring, centering them. Tie square knots around the beading wire to hide it. When you wish to add a bead, thread it onto the beading wire, and then tie square knots around it with the hemp strands.

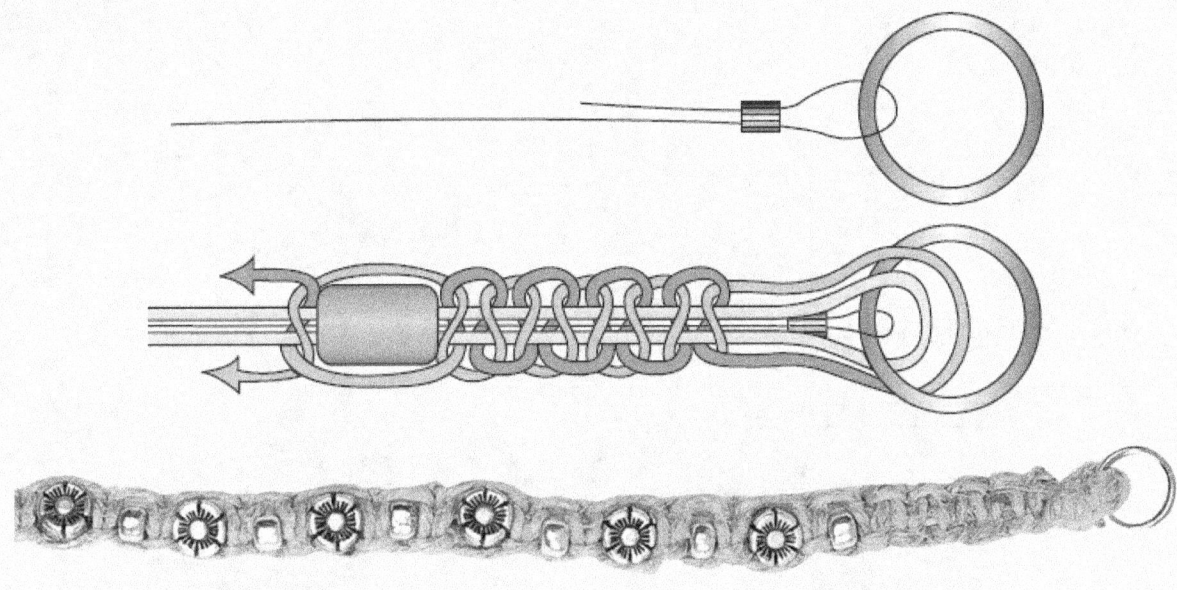

SQUARE KNOT VARIATIONS

Eight-strand alternating square knot with beads.

Four-strand alternating square knot

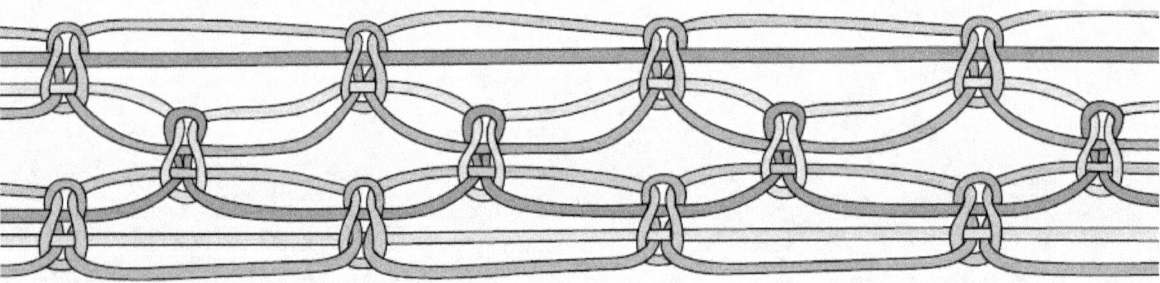

Eight-strand alternating square knot

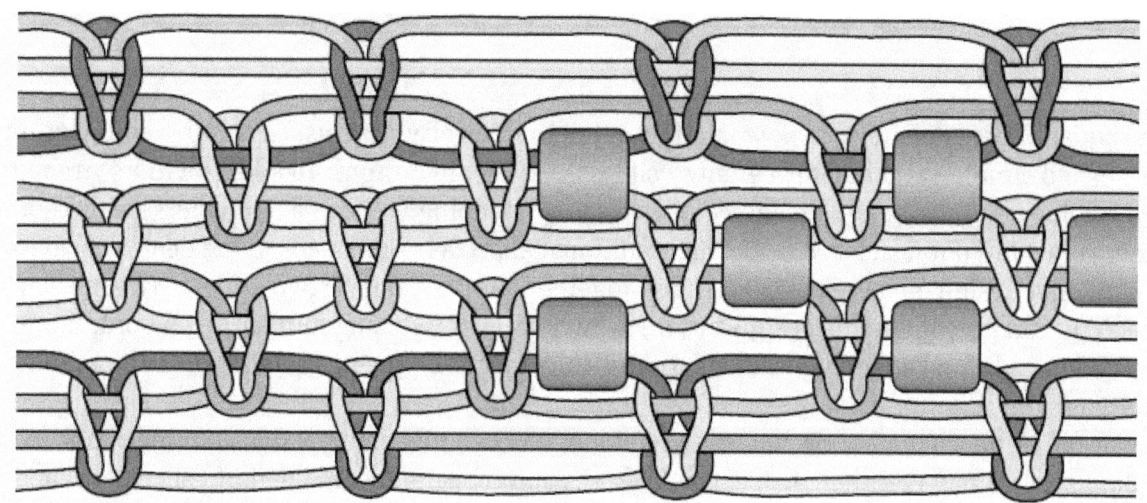
Twelve-strand alternating square knot

The square knot is one of the most familiar in knotted jewelry designs, as it is incredibly strong, dense, and simple to make. It is certainly a classic for hemp designs. In addition to its strength and stability, the square knot is incredibly versatile, meaning you can adapt your square knot designs to suit your taste. If you like the traditional approach, add beads to the center of your square knot design, placing the beads close together with just one or two knots between each one. You can give this same design a more grown-up look by using thinner hemp cord, more high-end beads, and attaching findings to finish the piece. Try using metallic cord for a really classy touch.

Because the square knot is not easily undone, you can give your designs a lighter look by adding space along their length. Tie square knots at the beginning and end of each space, and it will stay in place as long as you wear it. The number of strands in a square knot can be increased or decreased to change the look of the design. Go to six strands, and you can create scalloped edging. There are hundreds of designs you can make with just this knot alone. Do some experimenting and see what you can come up with!

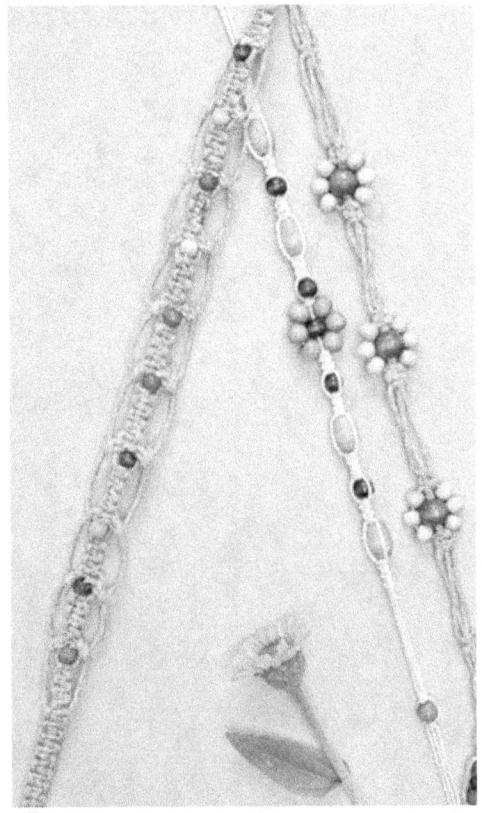

Make cute flower designs by adding a center bead to the center strands and three petal beads to each outer strand.

Try using six strands instead of four. You can use the outer two strands to create a scalloped design along the length of your piece as shown.

Leave space between your square knots. Try switching your outer working strands and center strands after each space to create a twisting design.

Add beads to one or both of the center strands and tie square knots around them with the working strands. Or, add beads to the outer working strands as shown in the far right bracelet design.

HALF KNOT TWIST

Half Knot Bracelet

Start with one 24" (61cm) strand and one 72" (183cm) strand of hemp, both doubled over for four strands total. Tie the strands together using an overhand knot with a ½" (1.5cm) loop at the top. Pull the knot tight and dot with glue if desired. Follow the illustrations to tie half knots around the short center strands with the long working strands until you reach the desired length. Thread beads onto both center strands as desired and tie half knots around them with the working strands. Finish with an overhand knot.

Bring the right working strand under the center strands and over the left working strand. Bring the left working strand over the center strands and under the right working strand.

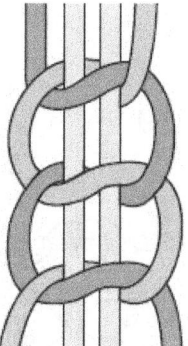

Repeat, always bringing the right strand under the center strands and over the left strand, and always bringing the left strand over the center strands and under the right strand.

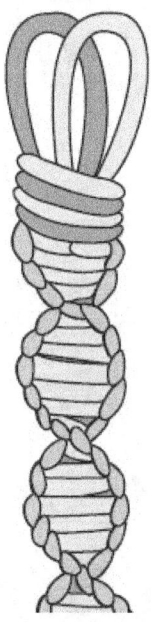

Tying the half knot will naturally cause the working strands to twist around the center strands as you go, forming a spiral shape.

HALF KNOT TWIST VARIATIONS

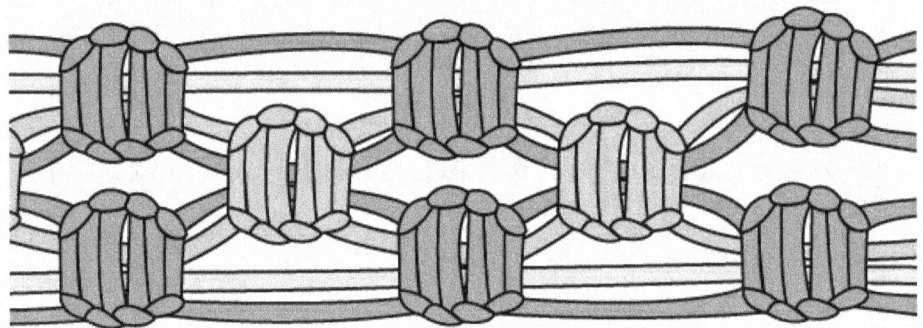

Eight-strand alternating half knot twist

Thread beads onto all the strands of your design to create a focal section.

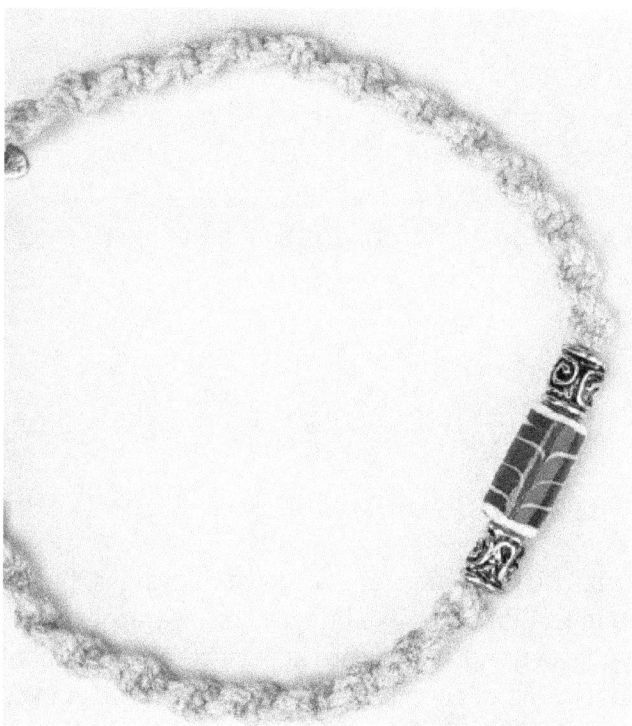

Rings join the half knot hemp section of this necklace with a multi-strand beaded section.

Beads can be added to your designs any way you want!

More STYLISH DESIGNS

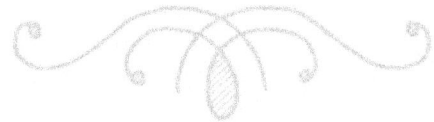

Exploring Fashionable Looks in New Materials

Embroidery floss and hemp are great materials for jewelry designs, but there are lots of other options out there for you to try. Products like bungee cord, paracord, and plastic lace are just a few of the many items you can use. Bungee cord is perfect for thick chunky projects. It can be knotted, beaded, or wrapped, and of course, it's stretchy! Paracord is excellent for knotted pieces, while plastic lace makes wonderful woven designs. Check out the projects on the following pages and be inspired to visit your local craft store and pick up a material you've never worked with before. Many of the designs shown use knots you have already encountered in this book. Check out the captions for helpful hints on creating your very own versions!

BUNGEE CORD

Thick bungee cord makes great chunky designs with a tribal feel, while thin bungee cord makes beautiful wrap bracelets. Keep it simple with a bead and a clasp or go wild with multiple strands, wraps, and beads.

Customize a simple bungee cord wrap bracelet by adding beads, dangles, and other accessories.

Large knots and braids look great in bungee cord. Try incorporating beads in your knotted designs.

Even on its own, bungee cord makes a big statement. Keep embellishments simple by adding one focal bead or a simple wrap.

PLASTIC LACE

Plastic lace has a wonderful sheen that looks great in jewelry designs. It comes in round and flat varieties and numerous colors. Take advantage of all the colors available to you when putting together your designs.

These bracelets have a simple woven design similar to those shown on this page.

Space out the center strands for a thicker design, or try creating a focal section by widening the strands when you reach the middle of the bracelet.

LIGHTWEIGHT PARACORD

Paracord is incredibly strong and durable, and it also makes beautiful jewelry designs. Try the thinnest variety of paracord (95) to knot, braid, or twist your own jewelry creations.

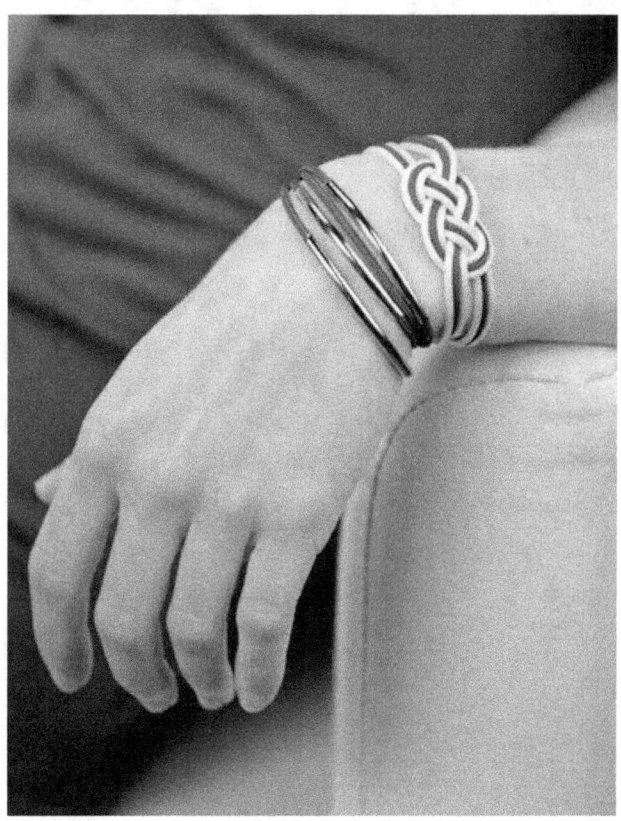

Friendship bracelet patterns look great in paracord. This bracelet uses stripes (this page), while the one below uses chevrons (this page).

Using thicker cord like paracord makes a French twist design (this page) really pop.

This six-strand alternating square knot design creates butterflies along the length of the bracelet. See Square Knot section for more about square knots for more about square knots.

MORE GREAT IDEAS

Anything that can be knotted, beaded, or wrapped can be turned into jewelry. Take a trip to your local craft store and see what you can find. From suede lace to metallic cord, there will always be something to spark your creativity!

Leather cord is a rich material that can lend sophistication to your jewelry. Create an elegant look with understated silver accents or a simple knotted design.

Metallic cord will give you all the sparkle you could ever want! Try adding cute accents like a tassel to pump up the fun. See this page for the stripe pattern.

Suede lace is soft and supple, making it perfect for jewelry. Stick with braids or flat knots for this material, like the modified carrick bend knot used for this bracelet.

www.ingramcontent.com/pod-product-compliance
Lightning Source LLC
Chambersburg PA
CBHW082209070526
44585CB00020B/2347